# TOUCHING THE
# HEART OF GOD

## CLEAN HANDS & A PURE HEART

Tracy Hogan

# OTHER BOOKS BY TRACY HOGAN

*The Good Shepherd's Heart: Living Parables*
Manifest International, LLC, 2019

*Bewitched & Beguiled: Wolves in Sheep's Clothing*
The Voice of My Beloved, 2021

# DEDICATION

This book is dedicated to the Lover of my soul—Yeshua, the only One Who is worthy of all of my love, time, devotion, adoration, worship, praise, thanksgiving and gratitude.  May our glorious Father and You, Yeshua, our magnificent, beautiful Savior—the King of kings and the Lord of lords alone be magnified and glorified throughout the pages of this book. May You, Yeshua, see the fruit of the travail of Your soul and be satisfied in every heart, who has ears to hear and eyes to see Your plans and purposes for their lives. May this book be an acceptable 'offering' of my undivided devotion to the only One who is holy, righteous, just and true in all of His ways—the only One called Faithful and True. AMEN!

# ACKNOWLEDGEMENTS

I want to thank those who have been nothing less than a source of strength and encouragement to me, as I embarked on the writing of this book. For I could not have done it without them!

Chelsea and Christine—forever thank you! No words could ever adequately express my deep love and eternal gratitude for all the ways that you have been nothing less than faithful, over and over again, to me and to the ministry, throughout the years. We have been through the fires and the floods together. Yet, despite it all your hearts still say, "Yes" to His plans and purposes that the Lord has as: spiritual daughters, as sisters, as beloved friends and as a ministry. Forever thank you for all the ways that you sow sacrificially: with your prayers, time and resources, using the gifts, talents and anointings that He has blessed you with to further His Kingdom on earth. Forever thank you for keeping the 'flame' burning, by keeping the watches going, enabling me to dedicate my time and focus to the writing of this book. You are truly my Aaron and Hur, for I could not have done it without you! I love you so much!

To the one who remains anonymous. Forever thank you for laying your holy eyes on every word and catching every little 'fox' possible! Bringing forth our heavenly assignments are like giving birth, and so grateful that you were willing to share some of the birthing pains with me, as you poured out your most excellent editing, all the while being my sounding board. Thank you for all your loving encouragement along the way, only wanting the very best for this book. The words on these pages shine forth much brighter because of you! I love you so dearly!

Mom, although your earthly role may have ended, forever thank you for praying for me, as you continue to fight the good fight of faith with us from heaven's viewpoint. I know that I could not have written this book, if you were not a part of the great cloud of witnesses, praying and cheering me on to finish the work the Father has ordained for me to do. I love you forever and ever!

Tanya, Jill, Mary, Kathy, Nancy, Mike, Tony and Tom, forever thank you for all your love, prayers, tears, encouragement and support, always! And especially during this time of writing. I am forever grateful for the eternal relationships and all that I have learned from your awesome and sacrificial walks with the Lover of our souls. I am honoured to travel the narrow road with each of you! Love you to the heavens!

# FOREWORD

Over the years as I read books, many of my conclusions are, "interesting topic," "there are some good ideas…" or, "I can see the writer's bend on this subject." This is a season where personal viewpoints pervade the digital bookshelves and where thought is subjective and myopic. This does not always allow for the wholistic understanding of the walk of called out ones.

*Touching the Heart of God* is a refreshing book that had me responding audibly many times at its content, whilst consuming the text. As I read, I quickly realized that it resonated from deep within my soul. What grabbed my spirit was the depth of biblical content that supported the subjects covered in the pages. The perspectives on the topic were clearly from the Father's perspective and not just the writer's thoughts.

This book is a manual for those who want to understand their walk with Jesus in a way that places Christ at the center of everything. One will understand that this read is prescriptive. If you take the content to heart and live by it as a priority in your life—your life will be transformed. If we choose not to live by these biblical principles, we will miss the intent the Father has for us.

Over the many years that I have known Tracy, her diligence in serving the Master has been profound. While her desire is to be invisible to the place where only Jesus is seen, her modeling of her devotion to the "Lover of her soul" cannot be ignored or misunderstood. As she incorporated a sensitive part of her personal story, I could not help but to be riveted and emotionally moved, yet it only pointed to the Source and not to Tracy.

*Touching the Heart of God* is a road map to a deep walk for the Bride of Christ that will bring Him pleasure. My conclusion is that I highly recommend this book. No matter where you are in your spiritual journey, you will learn and be touched by the transformational truth of the content.

REV. PAUL D.M JOHNSON D. MIN<br>
The Gathering Place Church<br>
Phoenix, Arizona, USA

# ENDORSEMENTS

On behalf of the Intercessors for the Philippines (IFP), a 35-year National Prayer Movement, I would like to endorse this book *Touching the Heart of God* by Tracy Hogan. Prayer and Intercession is our way of intimately communing with the Almighty, Holy and Loving God, to know His heart and His will, and ask Him to intervene in the affairs of men on the earth. This book wonderfully lays down what the Lord requires of us to be able to "ascend the hill of the Lord and stand in His holy place." Just like the priests in the Old Testament who have to do a lot of ceremonial preparations in approaching the presence of the Lord in the Tabernacle and the Temple, the author beautifully unveils to us the importance of the preparations of the condition of the heart, that of humility, holiness, brokenness and contriteness that the Lord requires from us.

Tracy powerfully highlights the urgency for God's people to be clothed with the bridal garment of purity and love and to passionately long to touch the heart of God, in this End Time season, as the Lord prepares His Bride and make ready His people for His coming Kingdom on the earth. May the Lord indeed raise up a generation of those who seek His face and be instruments of His redemption of every tribe, tongue, people and nation through prayers and intercession! I highly recommend this book to every pastor and intercessor who desire to touch the heart of God and who love to see the Lord's glorious appearing!

BISHOP DANIEL A. BALAIS
National Chairman, Intercessors for the Philippines (IFP)
Senior Pastor, Christ, the Living Stone Fellowship (CLSF)

I have known our dear sister Tracy Hogan for many years as a believer who thirsts for the deep things of God and as a member of the Bride of Christ who desires to beautify herself with the beauties of holiness. This book is the outcome of her personal life's pursuit of holiness, preparedness, and readiness to wait for and to be ready for the coming of the Lord Jesus.

The author has written in simple layman's terms what the Psalmist wrote in Psalms 15 and 24. The apostle Paul also wrote in the book of Hebrews that without holiness it is impossible to see God and caught away to be with the Lord when He comes for His Bride.

I highly endorse this book for every believer who desires to be made ready like the Bride who is waiting for her Bridegroom.

SADHU SUNDAR SELVARAJ
Jesus Ministries

In her newest book, Tracy has unpacked dozens of Scriptures that reveal the secret power of intercession, mingled with humility and painful obedience. She transparently shares the enormous price that the Lord's warriors pay, in the struggle to overcome the schemes of the enemy, both within our souls, and in our broken world.

In writing *Touching the Heart of God*, Tracy has articulately opened her own heart and shared with the reader the times of her deepest pain, loss, and brokenness in her life, the shattered hopes in her most precious relationships. But through humility, tears, prayer and costly obedience, we learn how powerfully the Lord will prove His faithfulness, even when we have waited so long.

I know this book will cut you to the heart, as you follow Tracy's journey through Scripture and through her sacrificial life. But it will open up new pathways of holiness and intimacy in your own walk and will encourage you to travail in prayer before our wonderful Lord, who will move on behalf of those who seek Him diligently.

JILL SHANNON
Author, Songwriter

This book ministered to me a lot. It pointed out areas in my life that need to be put right with God, so that I can pray and intercede alongside His will. I will study this book more thoroughly and teach it to our team. This is a book on consecrating ourselves unto sanctification. It is God's finishing school for His Remnants. The book outlines how to become one with our Father, in working alongside Him, and doing His will here on earth as it is in heaven. This book will be my study book for a season, until I overcome my personal issues with God. Thank you, Tracy.

WYDEN KING
Vision Keeper, NFS Foundation Ministry, Inc.
Makati City, Philippines

*Touching the heart of God* is an invitation to the Body of Christ to examine themselves and their walk with the Lord. Through her own experiences, Tracy reveals what are the keys to truly walk intimately with Yeshua and to touch His heart. This book will exhort the reader to repentance and a closer walk with our Savior. If you follow the keys revealed in this book, you can fulfill the Father's dream for you—to be restored back to the same place of intimate fellowship that Adam and Eve experienced in the Garden. He is just looking for a heart that wholeheartedly will say "Yes," no matter the cost.

ADEBANJO OLUWADARE
Scotland, UK

The end time spiritual battle is getting fiercer as the earth gets darker more than ever. The Bible declares that amid all this chaos, the Bride of Christ will arise, shine and be filled with His light and glory. This book will help equip the saints in becoming the glorious Bride of Christ triumphant in this last of the last days. I was tremendously blessed by Tracy's newest book *Touching the heart of God*. May the Lord continually enable and empower her in writing more books for Him to edify the saints and the entire Body of Christ.

REV. RUFFY PANALIGAN D. MIN
h.c. Jesus The Emmanuel Intercontinental Ministries
Brgy. Sucol, Calamba City, Laguna Philippines

This is a very timely book which every born-again believer must read and allow the message to penetrate our hearts. And afterwards to make our choice whether to stay in our comfortable place, or to go on to follow the Lamb and die to ourselves. The issues written about in this book are severely challenging. May we, His Body – the Church – rise to the occasion. It starts with each of us being willing. Is He worthy? Is He worth it?

MARY O'SULLIVAN<br>Lydia Leader Co. Kerry<br>Killarney, Ireland

How many times have you heard a person say, "I love the Lord?" How many times have we ourselves said it? Countless times, if we call ourselves Christians. It just rolls off the tongue without any deep thought as to what these words truly mean. We are Christians, so of course we "love" Jesus! But by whose standards? Tracy has laid out, in a very easy-to-read and applicable way, how to touch the heart of God. Her transparent stories from her own life, in how the Lord trained her, causes the reader to identify with the sufferings and joy that come when choosing to live a surrendered, crucified life unto the Lord.

I have had the privilege of walking through some testings, trials and promotions with Tracy. I can personally attest to her love, devotion, utter submission and obedience to whatever the Lord Yeshua calls her to do. I know it is her deepest desire and life goal to be conformed into the image of Christ, for she desires to see the Lamb receive the reward of His suffering. That desire drives her passion wanting to see each and every soul, who truly desires to walk with and please the Lord, come to that place of full-stature maturity in the Lord Yeshua.

As Tracy eloquently lays out, this place of touching His heart can only be accomplished through a life of prayer, from a sanctified and yielded heart. This is the only way, not only to get the attention of God, but to have our prayers answered. If you have a block in your prayer life, and or, have a desire to 'come up higher' — to be His Bride, and be used by the King through the gift of prayer, then I highly recommend this book for you.

TANYA NEWMAN
Intercessor
Pennsylvania, USA

Tracy Hogan has a divine mandate to release people, nations as well as individuals into their divine destiny. Tracy carries a special anointing to impart indispensable but profound truths and Kingdom principles with great simplicity, clarity and sharpness. In today's Christianity, when many fumble over the aspects of holiness, purity of heart and implicit obedience, through her new book *Touching the Heart of God*, Tracy has revealed the true heartbeats of our Father in heaven to every child of God, helping them to reach out to heaven's store room and Kingdom authority.

This book is a requisite for every believer, especially for the remnant, to finish their race victoriously.

BR. GEORGE JOHN
Jesus Ministries Europe
Widen, Switzerland

# CONTENTS


Introduction:   Touching the Heart of God ............................... xix

Chapter 1   The Bride's Invite .............................................1

Chapter 2   Obedience – Better Than Sacrifice ..................... 21

Chapter 3   The Robe of Humility & Meekness ..................... 37

Chapter 4   Renewal of the Mind ...................................... 51

Chapter 5   Holiness – Sanctified & Set Apart ..................... 67

Chapter 6   Called, Chosen & Faithful ............................... 85

Chapter 7   Our Prayers, Tears & Intercessions ................... 105

Chapter 8   Clean Hands & A Pure Heart ........................... 125

# TOUCHING THE HEART OF GOD

*Who may ascend into the hill of the Lord? Or who may stand in His holy place? He who has clean hands and a pure heart, who has not lifted up his soul to an idol, nor sworn deceitfully* [Psalm 24:3-4].

How we choose to live our lives impacts our prayer life either for good, or for bad. For out of the abundance of what is in our hearts will directly affect our communication and our walk with the Lord. And that relationship that we have with Him, depending on how pure our hearts are, will affect every other relationship we have – either for good, or for bad.

**MARK 7:21-23**
*For from within, out of the heart of men, proceed evil thoughts, adulteries, fornications, murders, thefts, covetousness, wickedness, deceit, lewdness, an evil eye, blasphemy, pride, foolishness. All these evil things come from within and defile a man.*

The Lord always goes straight to the heart of man when dealing with the sin in our lives and the multitude of character flaws that it brings. He wants to reveal truth that will set us free from bondage and restore purity to our soul, so that we can become compatible with

Him in our character. He wants us to complete the works that our Father has sent us to this earth to do, while displaying His character. For that is how the Son and the Father are glorified in and through our lives. He ultimately wants union with us, so that we may become One with Him. He wants to qualify us to reign with Him in the Millennium Reign [John 14:21, 17:4, 6, 21-23, Revelation 20:4-6].

1 Peter 1:15-16, says that we are to be holy, because He is holy. 1 John 2:6 further says that we ought to conduct our lives on this earth, as the Lord did when He walked this earth. And Matthew 5:48 reminds us to be perfect, as our Father in heaven is perfect [AP].

Often believers spiritualise verses like these away, instead of applying them to their lives literally. They believe or have been taught that we could never be like the Lord in our character, on this earth. But they could not be more wrong! The Lord always says what He means, and means what He says every time. He is not a cruel task master and He does not put commandments in His Word, if they were not possible to obtain. He does not play games with our lives. Instead, He calls us to lose our low life that we may obtain the high life. Verses like these are a call to surrender our will for His, in every area of our lives. And if we are willing, He will do the rest.

Years ago, after sharing how prayer and purity go hand in hand and how it is impossible to separate the two, someone wrote, asking to share more on what the Lord had shown me about prayer and intercession. Honestly, I was a bit surprised by this honest heart's precious words. I say that with all humility. I just could not see in my mind's eye how the two could be separate?

> **How could we define purity?** Freedom from foreign or inappropriate elements, anything that contaminates, pollutes, any admixture or modifying addition. Freedom from sin, guilt or evil; it is innocence, chastity, cleanness. The degree to which a color is free from being mixed with other colors, incapable of taint as gold of rust, without moral defects.[1]

The purer our hearts are, the more the Lord allows us to touch His heart. The Lord wants all of us to touch His noble heart. It is not an exclusive right for some and not for others. He is no respecter of persons. He created and longs to have intimate fellowship with us. He created us to co-partner with Him. We are all called to that deep place of intercessory prayer, it is not just for some. We will be the ones who decide how deep we go into His high, lofty and ever so noble heart by the choices we make and by the lifestyles we choose to live.

The Lord often touches our hearts with the Holy Spirit, wanting to awaken us out of our complacency and back to truth, purity and holiness. His desire is to draw us back to a pure, intimate relationship with Him and with the Father, so that we may clearly hear and obey His voice, for there is nothing more important for us to be doing. He did not create us to live a mundane, mediocre Christian life. Instead, we were created to live an extraordinary, supernatural life in Him. He wants us all to say, "Yes" to the Bride's invite, so that we may become One with Him and be filled with His glory and clothed in His Light. He wants us to be a testimony of His name, a testimony of His love, a testimony of His mercy and a testimony of His miracle working power to a lost world all around us who need a revelation of His Kingdom. But it all comes with a price tag attached. So, the question that we must ask ourselves; are we willing to pay the price? Do we even know what that price is and what it looks like in our lives?

Many Christians say they know Yeshua. But do they really? If you asked me, I would say, "No." To illustrate what I mean, I will use a public figure. If someone asked if I know President Trump, my initial response would be to say, *"Yes, of course, I know him!"* But the reality is that I only know of him. I do not know his personal likings, favorite foods etc. I do not know him well enough to call him on the phone or invite him to my home, or for him to invite me to his home. So the truth is, I do not know him, I only know of him. And that is how it is for most believers today. They do not really know the Lord; they only know of Him and do not even realise it! It breaks the Lord's heart greatly, for He died not just to save us from hell, but to reveal His heart and Kingdom ways that we may be One with Him.

If we are to get past the elementary stage in the teachings of Messiah and go on to perfection, and to know Him in order to touch His heart, we must rearrange our lives to come into alignment with His pure and holy ways. When we do, we will discover that He is much more available and accessible to us than any head of state or public dignitary! The Lord is passionate towards us, desiring to be with us far greater than we desire to be with Him. He will reveal as much of Himself as we want, but He has requirements. He has high standards where He is not going to lower them to meet our earthly idea of who we think He is, or how He should respond to us. That is the reality.

It will always be our choice in how well we get to know Him. And that 'knowing' will be determined by how much we are willing to lose our life, in exchange for His. Our prayer life is vital if we are to truly know Him and not just know of Him. I often say that prayer is heaven's love language. For it is how He chose to communicate with us, His created ones.

So, these awakenings that come into our lives are golden opportunities by the Master's design to purify our souls. Often these jolting's come through the relationships in our lives. For what better way to reveal what is really in our hearts than by those closest to us, and especially when things are not going so well. For out of the abundance of the heart the mouth speaks!

Daily, I ask the Lord to keep purifying my heart so I can touch His heart. So that I can love Him as He deserves. For the purer our hearts are the more that we can love Him, His way. I always thank Him for the purifying moments. I want them, I ask for them. I want to be able to touch His heart. For that is what true intercessory prayer is: touching the heart of God, causing the things that concern Him regarding the redemption of humanity to be fulfilled through yielded vessels.

Intercessory prayer is a positioning in Him, where we give of ourselves sacrificially all for Love's sake, not for our selfish gains, but for His heart to be appeased. For His eternal plans and purposes to manifest in and through His people, on earth as they exist in heaven. But that can only happen with those who are willing to be refined by fire; those who are in a relationship and a committed lifestyle of prayer with Him; those who are known as the Bride of Messiah—the Overcomers.

In that positioning we learn to be humble, to be corrected, and to let go of our ideas of what we think our lives are supposed to look like, sound like and feel like. The more we die to self by letting our souls be refined by fire and life's circumstances, the more our character becomes like His: love, joy, peace, patience, kindness, goodness, faithfulness, humility and self-control. We become more compatible with His character by one degree of glory after another, molding us into His likeness.

But whom the Lord allows to touch His heart is another story and it is not automatic. We can see this in Leviticus chapters 21-22. There were high requirements for the priests who ministered to the Lord in the Holy of Holies. It was not just anyone who could come before His altar with the burnt offering. They had to be without blemish. We are called to be kings and priests on this earth and if we are to walk effectively in our priestly roles, we must have clean hands and a pure heart.

**LEVITICUS 21:21-23**
*No man of the descendants of Aaron the priest, who has a defect, shall come near to offer the offerings made by fire to the Lord. He has a defect; he shall not come near to offer the bread of his God. He may eat the bread of his God, both the most holy and the holy; only he shall not go near the veil or approach the altar, because he has a defect, lest he profane My sanctuaries; for I the Lord sanctify them.*

**ISAIAH 57:15**
*For thus says the High and Lofty One Who inhabits eternity, whose name is Holy: I dwell in the high and holy place, with him who has a contrite and humble spirit, to revive the spirit of the humble, and to revive the heart of the contrite ones.*

Our ability to touch the heart of God will depend upon how willing we are to walk in humility before Him and others. And how willing we are to be completely broken by Him. Meaning, every part of our lives is to be filtered through Galatians 2:20, where we are crucified with Messiah. Where we no longer live for self, but for Messiah to live in and through us. Our humility and brokenness attract the Lord, along with our passion for Him. We see that passion in Luke 19 with Zacchaeus the tax collector. His passion got the Lord's attention, causing Him to come and stay with him [Matthew 5:5, Luke 19:1-5].

In August 2010, the Lord spoke to me about the state of His Church saying:

*"How she thinks she can mix her filth with His holiness. He is a high and Holy God, Who dwells in the highest of heavens! How so few would be His Bride, as His Bride will be without spot or wrinkle. They think they can mingle the Holy with their filth. I AM the Holy One Who sits in the highest heavens and I can only mingle with the pure."*

It is a word I will never forget. It is why I say that He does not allow everyone to touch His heart. He is not going to reveal His secrets— those things that are most precious to Him, and give His burdens for how we can comfort and appease Him through that place of intercessory prayer, if He cannot trust us with them.

It is the same in our human relationships. We do not share our most intimate details or sufferings with just anyone. Why? Because we do not want what is most precious to our hearts to be trampled upon, ignored, disregarded and treated with recklessness. How much more so with the Lord, for it is about souls being redeemed and nations' destinies being fulfilled. He tells us not to throw our pearls before swine and we can be sure neither will He! It is why our character must become compatible with His, if we want to become the Bride of Messiah, for His Bride will dwell in that deep place of intercession. When we do, we will only want what He wants and will do it His way, no matter what the cost to our lives.

Often, though, believers treat prayer recklessly with little, if any, heart preparation before they approach a holy God. By that I mean, we should be spending time before we come to church or a prayer meeting by asking the Lord to search our hearts and show us any wicked thing within us. And when He does, repent and make wrongs right where we can as fast as possible. When we do, we will come into His Sanctuary with cleans hands and a pure heart and will cause the manifest presence of God to be in our midst. Chains will come off, captives will be set free, lives will change! Instead, most believers are bringing the spirit of the world that dwells within their unrefined souls into these meeting times, often wanting to promote their own agenda.

Revelation 5:10 states we are called to be kings and priests. But our priestly garments must be clean. That speaks of our hearts, our thoughts, how we treat others, and our motives. They all must be pure, if we are to touch His heart and to be His Bride [Psalm 24:3-4, Revelation 19:7-9].

Many like to walk in their kingly roles, declaring and decreeing, but few walk in that position with pure heart motives. Instead, hearts are full of pride, selfish gain, deceit, lusts, impure thoughts, offenses, anger, envy, greed, sexual sin, unforgiveness, it goes on and on.

But prayer from a humble heart that hungers for truth starts the Bridal process in our lives. Often what I call our journey to becoming His Bride. For it is how we get to know His noble heart in order to become like Him. Prayer is communion with the Lover of our soul. Without it, we cannot know Him and we will be left fully dissatisfied, as we will only know of Him. For without prayer, we cannot know His likes and His dislikes or heaven's protocols that we are to follow.

Prayer causes our hard hearts to become soft towards Him. Because, as we draw near to Him, He draws near and comes with His Light and lightens our dark souls, so we can see our hearts the way He does. As His Light penetrates our darkness, we want to be cleansed—to be pure. We will want to get rid of our spots, wrinkles and blemishes, because we will see Him as He really is and want to be like Him [1 John 3:2-3].

Prayer is a call to come before Him without our agendas. It is a call to be selfless, sacrificial, where we want only His burdens prayed through us. And that requires us to come before Him in purity, in humility and out of lovesick obedience, and not out of compulsion. Once in this Bridal position, the Lord will share His secrets and trust us to steward and accomplish His purposes for mankind. We see this with Abraham and Lot when the Lord said, *"Shall I hide from Abraham, what I am about to do?"* Abraham was God's friend and he was a powerful intercessor. Why? Because God knew Abraham as His own kind and that he would obey and follow the Lord wholeheartedly. The Lord shares His secrets with His friends, but He gets to qualify who His friends are, not us, and not everybody is His friend [Genesis 18:17, 19, Isaiah 41:8, 2 Chronicles 20:7, John 15:14].

The Lord is calling us all much higher! It is why I say it is impossible to separate prayer from purity and how they go hand in hand. And when working together, they cause our relationship with the Lord to grow and mature. For it is this deep place of prayer, intimacy and purity where the Lord will reveal His plans, strategies and purposes for how we are to co-labor with Him. It cannot be revealed any other way. For it is in this intimate, consecrated prayer and Word life, where we will get the revelation that we need to successfully fulfill the call that is on our lives.

This is how true transformation takes place in a believer's life: first, a surrendering, with a purifying, then a commissioning takes place. It is why Satan tries to destroy our prayer life any way that he can: distractions, fear, sin, doubt, sickness, fatigue, depression, by things that appear good but are misleading and really futile, or by worldly activity. Satan fears a praying Remnant for he knows that prayer coming from pure, consecrated vessels will cause his plans to fail, ultimately to his final defeat.

It is why intercession, this deep place of intimate prayer is vital more than ever in this late hour as we see an acceleration of darkness coming upon the nations. Equally, it must come forth from a position of purity in vessels who will be known as the 'crucified ones,' for they will go through the fiery trials of affliction and come out pure gold, molded and shaped into His very likeness. This Bridal company will walk in 'unoffended love,' pushing back the darkness in these last days, all for His glory to shine in and through them. And all for the Lamb to see the fruit of the travail of His soul and be satisfied through these surrendered hearts, who are willing to follow Him wholeheartedly, so that the nations may be saved!

This book is written to and for the Bride of Messiah. It is for those who will overcome by the blood of the Lamb, by the word of their testimony and who will not love their own life, unto death. It is for those who are hungering and thirsting for a deeper, more intimate walk with the Lover of their soul, and who are dissatisfied with the lukewarm and ordinary. It is for those who will say, "Yes" to the Bride's Invite to help them better understand the price to be paid.

As you read this book, may you be encouraged, provoked and built up in every way that the enemy has tried to steal, kill and destroy God's plans for your life. May it cause you not to give in, give up or give over to Satan's lies that he has whispered into your ears telling you that it is too late, and nothing will ever change for you. Instead, may you know that you have been called and chosen for such a time as this, for you are His best wine that He has saved for these last days! May it be settled, deep within your soul, that you are called to be His Bride. A Bride who will labor with one hand and know how to wield your sword effectively with the other hand, all the while keeping your hands clean and your heart pure. AMEN!

# CHAPTER 1

# THE BRIDE'S INVITE

*There are sixty queens and eighty concubines, and virgins without number; But my dove, my undefiled and perfect one, stands alone [above them all]; she is the only one of her mother, she is the choice one of her who bore her. The daughters saw her and called her blessed and happy, yes, the queens and the concubines, and they praised her. Let us be glad and rejoice and give Him glory, for the marriage of the Lamb has come, and His wife has made herself ready. And to her it was granted to be arrayed in fine linen, clean and bright, for the fine linen is the righteous acts of the saints. Then he said to me, "Write: 'Blessed are those who are called to the marriage supper of the Lamb!' And he said to me, "These are the true sayings of God." And I saw the beast, the kings of the earth, and their armies, gathered together to make war against Him who sat on the horse and against His army* [Song of Solomon 6:8-9 Amp., Revelation 19:7-9, 19].

## Wedding and a War

The Lord is coming back soon, first for a wedding, and then a war against the kings of this earth that have fought against Him.

That war will usher in the Millennium Reign where the King of kings will restore His Kingdom on this earth with His Bride by His side for 1,000 years. We see prior to the Wedding Supper of the Lamb taking place, in Revelation 3:16-18, that the Lord exhorts us to purchase gold refined by fire. Every believer should be in what I call bridal and war preparation, where we are allowing the Lord to remove every spot, wrinkle or any such thing from our souls and from our lifestyles, while staying engaged in the battle, fighting the good fight of faith with our intercessory prayers to push back the darkness that threatens to destroy us, our families, our communities, our cities and nations. It requires our response every day. It has to be intentional, if we want to possess our full inheritance, which is to be the Bride of Messiah.

At the same time, we need to understand that there is a wedding for us to attend. That all in the Body are invited, but not all will be chosen to attend the Marriage Supper of the Lamb, for it requires us to obtain pure and spotless garments and obtaining those garments are not automatic at our new birth. In fact, obtaining those garments will cost us everything, meaning losing our lives – the low life, in order to find the high life, which can only come about if we are willing to deny ourselves, take up our cross and follow the Lamb [Matthew 22:11-14, 16:24-26].

Most in the Church are not aware of the Lord's Feast of all feasts— the Wedding Supper of the Lamb; therefore, they are not preparing for it. They believe or have been taught that it is automatic for all believers to be the Bride of Messiah. If there is not a realignment of their priorities to be Kingdom minded, and not focused on the temporal – the me, I and self, they will miss the very purpose for which God created them. They might make it to heaven, but will miss fulfilling their high and lofty destiny to be the Bride of Messiah and to rule with Him during the Millennium Reign. That is a promise only to the Overcomers and not automatic for all believers. It is a promise to those who have overcome by the blood of the Lamb, by the word of their testimony and who have not loved their own life, unto death [Revelation 3:21, 12:11, 20:4-6].

The Lord is looking for a company of people whom He can inhabit, in every area of their souls. A habitation where He can fill them with His glory and clothe them with His Light. That habitation will take place in vessels who will receive the end result of their faith, the salvation of their souls; those who are willing to be emptied of self and the spirit of this world in order to be prepared for His soon Second Coming, and return [1 Peter. 1:9].

Why, you might ask is this important? Because it is the Lord's answer for the dark days that are upon us, not only to endure them, but to overcome them His way. So that every soul and every nation that can be saved, will be saved, for that is the reward of His suffering. He will do this with His Bride, who will co-partner with Him to bring in the great harvest during the great tribulation, and then co-partner with Him, restoring righteousness on this earth, during the Millennium Reign [Matthew 24:13, Psalm 2:8, Revelation 2:26-27, 11:15, 14:15-16, 20:4-7].

## Pre-tribulation Rapture: Fact or Fiction?

If we are to be prepared for the Wedding and the war that is coming and not lose our eternal rewards that the Lord has for us, we must understand that there is no early escape clause for His Church. In the book of Daniel, we see there is a final seven-year period of testing for those who are left on the earth during this time, and before the Lord's return. The first three and a half years of this period, Scripture does not reveal much about what will happen, during those years of tribulation [Daniel 9:27].

But we see that when the abomination that makes desolate takes place midpoint, we will have entered into what some scholars describe as the great tribulation. The Lord also spoke about the great tribulation in Matthew 24:21-22, telling us that if those days had not been shortened no one would survive. But for the sake of the elect, those days have been shortened. He further said, it would be *after* the tribulation – not before, when the Son of Man would appear in the sky and send out His angels with a loud trumpet call to gather His elect [Daniel 11:31, Matthew 24:29-31].

So a very good case can be made that the Church will be here for all seven years, where the last three and a half years will be where we will see affliction, distress, sufferings and oppression as never before seen on the earth. The Lord could shorten that time, but we cannot count on that or expect that to happen. Instead, we must prepare to endure to the end that we may be saved.

**MATTHEW 24:13**
*But he who endures to the end shall be saved.*

Pre-tribulation Rapture teachings have caused a slumber to come upon the masses and to be quite divisive. Those who believe in this doctrine, believe that all Christians will be raptured right before the seven-year tribulation period begins, and will not have to suffer with those who are left on the earth at that time. If one would really stop to think about it, would that really be the Lord's heart, to take all believers off the earth right before the anti-Christ sets up his throne to rule over the nations, and let the rest of humanity perish in his hands? What hope will they have? Who will lead them to the Way, the Truth and the Life? Who is going to display His miracle working powers and do great exploits that Daniel spoke about in chapter eleven? Who will help Him bring in the harvest? For the truth is that people will be getting saved, and believers will be martyred for Messiah—those who refuse to take the Mark of the Beast, during this time period.

I believe that the pre-tribulation Rapture doctrine is a Christian mindset that does nothing to promote God's plans for our lives on this earth, which includes being prepared to endure this time. For those who do embrace the pre-tribulation Rapture doctrine, they do not understand the heart of God, for whatever reasons. They do not understand the promises that are given only to those who overcome; these are mentioned in Revelation chapters 2 and 3. They do not understand what He will bring forth from His Bride during this very difficult and traumatic time, and how the Lamb is going to shine brightly in that bridal company that Isaiah 60:1-2 speaks about.

The Lord will be magnified and glorified in and through them. Many believers do not understand that the Lord is going to use this time to bring forth a pure and spotless Bride.

But how merciful is our Lord to limit that time period! For that we can only give thanks forever, for His mercy endures forever! As a believer, we are not appointed to wrath, but we are told that it is with much hardship and tribulation that one must enter the Kingdom of God. The Remnant – the Bride of Messiah, will be on this earth during the great tribulation. It is going to be the Lord's greatest moment to be glorified, in all of humanity, and no man is going to steal that glory from Him, for He will not share His glory with another, nor His praise with idols. To think that God would take all believers off the earth, right when His biggest harvest will come, is short-sighted and does nothing to cause people to prepare for the difficult days ahead. Revelation 3:10, 13:10, 14:12 and 20:4 indicate that believers will still be here for the tribulation.

Daniel 12:10 speaks of those who will come forth and be purified during this time. This will be His Bride who will finally make herself ready. He is not coming one second before she has made herself ready, and He will use the tribulation to help her get ready. He loves us that much to do so, not wanting anyone to miss out on being able to rule with Him for eternity. The Lord wants us prepared, not troubled or fearful of this time, but ready to go through the fire like never before, knowing that His grace is sufficient and that He is fighting for us and not against us!

**DANIEL 12:10**
*Many shall be purified, made white, and refined, but the wicked shall do wickedly; and none of the wicked shall understand, but the wise shall understand.*

When the shout of the Bridegroom goes out at midnight, this is when His Bride will be "caught up" and the Marriage Supper will take place. It will be for those who have made themselves ready. This is the first resurrection that Revelation 20:5-6 exhorts us to be a part of, but states that not everyone who is in the Body of Messiah will be a part of it.

> **REVELATION 20-5-6**
> *But the rest of the dead did not live again until the thousand years were finished. This is the first resurrection. Blessed and holy is he who has part in the first resurrection. Over such the second death has no power, but they shall be priests of God and of Christ, and shall reign with Him a thousand years.*

In Daniel 11:32 we see hope! In midst of the tribulation, a company of people are standing strong and doing great exploits. These are the Overcomers, the Sons of God, the Bride of Messiah, who have made themselves ready. It is those who know their God intimately, by dying to self and who have become a living sacrifice for the gain of Messiah [Galatians 2:20, Romans 12:1-2.]

If we are to be the Bride and be prepared for the Wedding Supper of the Lamb, then we have to address this issue that has caused a great slumber upon His people. The purpose of this book is not to do an in-depth study on this very complex topic. The purpose of this book it to help us to be a Bride, one who will endure to the end. What I have shared does not go into the depth of this topic, but you can listen to a teaching that I did titled, *The Days of Noah*,[2] on our website, Rumble or YouTube channel, where I laid a foundation from scriptures to dispel the lie of pre-tribulation Rapture. Or, you may want to read Dr. Michael L. Brown's and Craig S. Keener's book, *Not Afraid of the Antichrist: Why We Don't Believe in a Pre-Tribulation Rapture*,[3] where they analyse this topic in every detail possible, based on Scripture.

## Bridal Terminology

The word bride, bridegroom and bridal chamber is referenced over 40 times in the Bible. For men, who are challenged being called a bride, which is normally feminine in the natural way of life, be assured that this has nothing to do with our physical gender, but it speaks of spiritual maturity. These words are His terminology, not man's, so the sooner we understand that the Lord is not trying to strip our men of their masculinity, the better. Instead, it all has to do with being found in the right wedding garment – not dress! It is interesting to note that the Hebrew word "callah" in the Bible means: a bride as perfect, Strong's 3618.[4]  It is taken from the Hebrew root word "calal" which means: to complete, make perfect, Strong's 3634.[5] We can see that the purpose and the plan of God has always been in His Word – to have a Bride, who is made perfect for His Son!

## The Wedding Invite Parable

Let us take a closer look at Matthew 22, where we see the parable of the Wedding Banquet. When we read this parable, we need to keep in mind the Lord is speaking to believers, not the unsaved, which will become clear as we look at each verse in detail.

> **MATTHEW 22:2-14 AMP.**
> *The kingdom of heaven is like a king who gave a wedding banquet for his son,[3] And sent his servants to summon those who had been invited to the wedding banquet, but they refused to come.[4] Again he sent other servants, saying, tell those who are invited, Behold, I have prepared my banquet; my bullocks and my fat calves are killed, and everything is prepared; come to the wedding feast.[5] But they were not concerned and paid no attention [they ignored and made light of the summons, treating it with contempt] and they went away—one to his farm, another to his business,[6] While the others seized his servants, treated them shamefully, and put them to death.[7] [Hearing this] the king was infuriated; and he sent his soldiers and put those murderers to death and burned their city.[8] Then he said to his servants, The wedding*

*[feast] is prepared, but those invited were not worthy.[9] So go to the thoroughfares where they leave the city [where the main roads and those from the country end] and invite to the wedding feast as many as you find.[10] And those servants went out on the crossroads and got together as many as they found, both bad and good, so [the room in which] the wedding feast [was held] was filled with guests.[11] But when the king came in to view the guests, he looked intently at a man there who had on no wedding garment.[12] And he said, Friend, how did you come in here without putting on the [appropriate] wedding garment? And he was speechless (muzzled, gagged).[13] Then the king said to the attendants, tie him hand and foot, and throw him into the darkness outside; there will be weeping and grinding of teeth.[14] For many are called (invited and summoned), but few are chosen.*

In order to understand this parable in context, it is vital not to gloss over verse 2, where the Lord says, *"The Kingdom of heaven is like a king who gave a wedding banquet for his son."* And we must understand what a kingdom is and how one functions. In the natural, a kingdom is a piece of land that is ruled by a king or a queen. It is often called a monarchy, which means that one person, usually inheriting their position by birth or marriage, is the leader or head of state.

Kingdoms are one of the earliest types of societies on earth, dating back thousands of years. Today, there are still a few kingdoms that are ruled by an absolute monarch. King Salman bin Abdulaziz Al Saud of Saudi Arabia, King Mswati III of Swaziland, and King Hassanal Bolkiah of Brunei are absolute monarchs. All of these kingdoms have legislatures and sets of laws. The monarch remains the final authority.[6] In earlier time periods, it was the king's responsibility to take care of all of his subjects' needs. If a person was not a part of his monarchy, they could not dwell within it, and they had no benefits from it.

So, we see in verse 2 that the Kingdom of heaven is a monarchy, where the King's subjects dwell, who are under the King's rule and are expected to obey His laws. That applies to anyone who has received the free gift of salvation. When we did, we agreed to His terms. With His blood, He paid a price to own us, where we no longer can do whatever we want. He expects us to obey His Word and commandments. If we do, He will go above and beyond what is needed to take care of our needs. It is that understanding that we need to have when reading this jolting parable.

**In verse 2:** The King is the Father, who is going to have a Wedding Supper for His Son, Yeshua. Refers to Revelation 19:7, the Wedding Supper of the Lamb.

**In verse 3:** His servants, whom He sent to summon those who had been invited, depict those who have gone before us, and those in this last generation who are called to help prepare the Bride of Messiah: apostles, prophets, evangelists, pastors and teachers. Those that refused to come are believers who rejected their teachings on truth, purity, holiness, and what is required to be the Bride of Messiah. He is still sending servants today, to those invited—His people, but most are refusing. This shows a condition of their hearts. They are hard, rebellious and complacent. Remember that He is a King, who dwells in a Monarchy, and He is first giving this invitation to His own people, He wants the very best for them!

**In verse 4:** He sends more servants to those invited— to believers, emphasising that everything is ready, come! This depicts how patient, merciful and gracious the Father is to us. He wants all to be prepared, to come and not miss the Banquet. It reveals that everything is ready for the Wedding Supper to take place, except His Bride!

**In verse 5:** They ignored and made light of the invitation, and treated it with contempt. Today, likewise, at large, the Body is not concerned about purity and holiness. They have lost the fear of the Lord, causing them to pay no heed to the call to be prepared and to be found in the right garments. Most are asleep, content with being lukewarm and do not even know they are lukewarm. They are doing what seems good and right in their own minds, and much of their conduct is purposeless [2 Peter 1:8].

**In verse 6:** Shows how those sharing this message, by inviting those to come and to be the Bride of Messiah, are treated shamefully by other believers. Some being put to death, speaks not only of martyrdom for preaching the Gospel that Yeshua, the Apostles and Paul preached—the crucified life, but it also points to believers, who have destroyed the reputation of true minsters of God who gave them this hard message.

**In verse 7:** When the Father heard about what had been done to His faithful servants, He was furious! His jealous love will avenge His Bride, and those who have been faithful to help prepare her for His Son. And those who have refused the invitation and brought harm to His faithful servants will face the loss of eternal rewards. For vengeance is His to repay and we can be certain that He will mete out to each one of us as our deeds deserve.

**In verse 8:** We see the Wedding Banquet is ready. The believers who refused the invitation, He tells them they are not worthy to be His Son's Bride. By declining the invite to die to self, and let the Lamb live in and through them, they are telling the King, He is not worth knowing, therefore the King says they are not worthy. These are hard words, but we see the grace of God in His Word, not wanting anyone to miss His eternal plans for our lives. Remember Queen Vashti, who refused to come to King Ahasuerus' banquet. She rebelled and held her own banquet. Because of it, she was no longer queen and replaced by Esther, who only wanted what the King wanted for her life. Prior to becoming queen, Esther spent 12 months being purified before she came before the king. If we are to be the Bride, we must be making ourselves ready.

**In verse 9:** Everything is ready, except the Bride! If His own people will not accept the invitation, it now goes out to the highways and byways. It goes out to everyone, including the unsaved. The invitation to be His Son's Bride was first to the Church, now to the rest of the world. This parable was not an invitation to receive salvation. You already have to be saved, to belong to the Kingdom. It is vital that we do not miss this truth. It is a grave warning for all believers. For He now bypasses them and sends His servants to invite anyone who will listen and obey.

**In verse 10:** His servants shared the wedding invitation with as many as they could find, good and bad and the wedding hall was filled. This depicts the Church today, where the wheat and tares are gathered in one place.

**In verse 11:** We see the King comes to view "the guests" and He looks *intently* at a man who does not have on the right "wedding garments." This speaks of how the King will scrutinize our works. Did we do our will or His will? Did we build our kingdom or His Kingdom? Did we use the gifts and the anointings for selfish gain? Did we become love, and the fruit of the Spirit? Were we willing to purchase gold refined by fire and eye salve that we might see the spots, wrinkles and blemishes that needed removed from our words, thoughts and deeds?

**REVELATION 19:8**
*And to her it was granted to be arrayed in fine linen, clean and bright, for the fine linen is the righteous acts of the saints.*

**In verse 12**: The King asks, *"Friend, how did you come in here without putting on the [appropriate] wedding garments?"* Note that the man was speechless with no excuses. It was because he knew that he had been given many opportunities to prepare, but he had refused. It required his response "to put on the right garment" and he chose not to do it. Yeshua says there is only one way to enter the sheepfold, and if anyone tries to come in any other way, they are a thief and a robber [John 10:1]. Likewise, there is only one way to become the Bride of Messiah and that is by taking up our cross constantly, until our flesh has been crucified. In that process of dying, we learn to recognise the Bridegroom's voice, and how to dress ourselves in our "wedding garments." These garments signify our purity, holiness, righteousness, just and consecrated lifestyles, deeds and conduct, where we will live a surrendered life unto the Lamb, and have dove's eyes for Him alone.

**In verse 13:** The King has the man thrown out into outer darkness. The King alone defines what is required to be His Bride, not us!

**In verse 14:** Many are called, few are chosen. We saw how all were invited to attend the Wedding Banquet, but how few accepted the invitation. It is why I say, all in the Body are not the Bride, but the Bride is a part of the Body. Most believe they are automatically the Bride, because they believe in Yeshua. But that is not what Scripture teaches, nor what the Lord demonstrates for us in this parable.

When reading this parable, have you ever wondered why someone would want to kill the person who had invited them to a wedding? Normally, a wedding is a joyous occasion and who could take offense at being invited to one? It is because it is a hard message to hear. It means giving up everything in a person's life and to come out of all compromise, mixture and worldly desires in order to attend. It is the message of the crucified life – deny ourselves, take up our cross and follow the Lamb. For the believers who have been seduced by the false prosperity teachings, which tells them they do not have to suffer, and that God just wants them happy, rich, comfortable and that they are in no need of repentance, this would put quite a monkey wrench into their ideology.

## No Spots, Wrinkles or Any Such Things!

Revelation 19:7-8 tells us that His Bride has prepared herself. The Marriage Supper of the Lamb is for His Bride who has made herself ready on this earth, today, and she has a very active role to play, every day, every choice she makes. The Lord is only going to accept a Bride whose heart is pure and wholehearted towards Him, meaning: no other lovers, but of single devotion and without spots or wrinkles. Peter speaks of how we should be found on this earth before the Lord returns, that we are to be without spot or blameless.

### 2 PETER 3:10-11, 13-14
*But the day of the Lord will come as a thief in the night, in which the heavens will pass away with a great noise, and the elements will melt with fervent heat; both the*

*earth and the works that are in it will be burned up. Therefore, since all these things will be dissolved, what manner of persons ought you to be in holy conduct and godliness, Therefore, beloved, looking forward to these things, be diligent to be found by Him in peace, without spot and blameless;*

**2 CHRONICLES 16:9**
*For the eyes of the Lord run to and fro throughout the whole earth, to show Himself strong on behalf of those whose heart is loyal to Him.*

**EPHESIANS 5:25-27**
*Husbands, love your wives, just as Christ also loved the church and gave Himself for her, that He might sanctify and cleanse her with the washing of water by the word, that He might present her to Himself a glorious church, not having spot or wrinkle or any such thing, but that she should be holy and without blemish.*

In Revelation 3:20, the Lord is standing and knocking on the door of every believer's heart. He is saying, if anyone hears My voice and opens the door, I will come in to him and dine with him, and he with Me. This is not a call to salvation, but an invitation to let the Lord come and show us our spots, wrinkles and blemishes, and to be cleansed from them so that we can be restored back to an intimate relationship with Him and with the Father. Prior to this invitation to come and dine with us, we see in Revelation 3:18-19 that we are exhorted to purchase from Him gold "refined and tested by fire" that we would be clothed in white garments. Our sin separates us from intimate fellowship with Him and from being able to fulfill our destinies. The goal of the Father's discipline in our lives is to bring us back into obedience to His Word and righteous ways so that the eternal plans and purposes for our lives can be fulfilled.

## Gold Refined by Fire

To purchase "gold" speaks of our hearts being naked before the One Whose eyes are flames of fire. Practically, it means we should be crying out every day, *"Search my heart O God and show me anything wicked within me."* And when He does, we need to be quick to repent and obey. We must earnestly pursue to turn from our ways and lifestyle choices that were never His way for us. In the natural, impurities in gold are removed by intense heat. The heat melts the metal, causing the impure to be separated from the pure. When the process is complete, the end result is "pure gold." This speaks of the process that our hearts go through when the Refiner's fire comes into our lives through the trials, testings and afflictions.

**ISAIAH 48:10**
*Behold, I have refined you, but not as silver; I have tried and chosen you in the furnace of affliction.*

How we respond to suffering in our lives will determine how much we allow the Master's Refiners fire to purify us. We can be certain that He will be faithful to bring our "custom designed" tests, trials, and afflictions that are needed to purify our souls of every spot, wrinkle and blemish that we may be His Bride. Their purpose is to expose the "tares" of our hearts that need to be uprooted, so our character can be conformed into His likeness. That should be every believer's number one priority in life, having Messiah completely formed within their soul. We do not want to waste our trials and tears; instead, we want to embrace them!

Our sufferings are meant to transform us, not destroy us. Yeshua and Paul understood this intimately. Yeshua being our ultimate example. His sacrificial death brought resurrection power that raised Him back to life, back to glory! So too, is His plan for us, if we are willing to die to self. When we do, He can resurrect His plans in our lives, while preparing us to rule with Him forever.

## Pure, Holy Intimacy

The Lord declares the end from the beginning and He is in the process of restoring all things. He is restoring a company of people, a bridal company, who are known as the Overcomers, the Sons of God, back to the Garden of Eden to that same place of pure, holy intimacy that Adam and Eve walked in before the fall of man. They were filled with His glory and clothed in His Light. This is His plan for us, on this earth, not when we get to heaven. Revelation 3:10 is not an escape clause. It is a promise to protect His Bride from the hour of trial that is coming upon the whole world, when the anti-Christ sets up his throne to rule over the nations. He will use this company of people mightily to bring in the Harvest during this time [Isaiah 46:10, Acts 3:21, Revelation 3:10, 13:5-7].

This holy intimacy is developed, nurtured, matured and maintained with a lifestyle of prayer and reading and meditating on the Word. Without a consecrated lifestyle of prayer, we will always judge the Word of God with our mind. When we come into deeper intimacy with the Bridegroom, we begin to know the Father's perfect love that casts out all fear. We will not fear the shakings and darkness around us. Instead, will be His love and light setting captives free from it. We will know that the Lord is on our side, we will not fear, for what can man do to us [Psalm 118:6].

Genesis to Revelation is about a wedding taking place, and the restoration of God's family. It is about the Father having a Bride for His Son that will be worthy of Him and to be the Lamb's wife – meaning equally yoked to Him in word, thought and deed, having been perfected in love. But if we do not know what our faith is meant to obtain, we will wander aimlessly missing the high call that is on our lives to be the Bride, never fulfilling our destiny. Equally, we must know, God will never understand our disobedience. We all have access to the same Holy Spirit and He will freely give as much grace that we need to obey and to be corrected.

## The Invitation is Optional

Remember, an invitation to attend an event is optional. We can either accept or decline the invitation. The choice will always be ours to make. Back in 2010, my invitation to be His Bride came after an extended period of intense purification. I wrote about this time in detail in *Bewitched & Beguiled: Wolves in Sheep's Clothing.*[7] What I did not share, was moments before the Lord gave me that hard word to hear about the condition of His people's hearts, *"...where they think they can mingle the Holy with their filth,"* He asked, *"Will you come, be My Bride?"* I said, *"Yes."* The Lord then spoke saying, *"There is a high price, it is costly."* I told Him that I did not care what it would cost me, that He was worth everything. He was letting me know that it was costly, and the choice would be mine. He has been faithful to that word. Thus far, it has cost me everything!

It is why I share with others that it will cost you everything, if you are to become the Bride of Messiah. There is much misunderstanding about what God requires, and what costing everything really means. Luke chapter 14 verses 26-27 and 33 help us better understand the cost, if we are to be a true disciple of Messiah.

We saw in the Wedding Banquet parable how the King reached out many times to invite His own people. I believe He did, because He is full of grace and truth and wants to give us every opportunity to accept it. But He will not force it on anyone. Instead, He desires that we would all want to be His Bride. The King's standards are high and holy and not everyone will qualify to be the Bride. He is not looking to disqualify anyone. Most will disqualify themselves by the choices they make, if not willing to live a consecrated, 100% surrendered life unto the Lord.

We see that with the ten virgins who took their lamps and went to meet the Bridegroom. The ten virgins depict believers, not unsaved people. The five wise virgins were prepared, they had oil in their lamps. The five foolish virgins had no oil in their lamps, they were not prepared. The oil speaks of our relationship with the Lord. It speaks of what we have invested in that relationship in order to know Him and to be known by Him.

The five foolish had wanted the five wise to give them some of their oil and they told them to go purchase their own. We cannot give someone else our relationship that we have with the Lord. It is why they had to go buy it and pay the price for it themselves. Because they had wasted their time up to that point to do so, when the midnight cry came that the Bridegroom had come, only the five wise went into the Wedding and the door was shut. When the five foolish tried to get the Lord to open the door, He told them, *"I say to you, I do not know you."* They did not make it to the Wedding because they were not prepared [Matthew 25:1-11].

## Time is Running Out!

Time is running out. The hour is very late and most in the Church are like the five foolish virgins, asleep with very little oil in their lamps. We are coming into some very difficult times that we have not seen before this age. We must be a people who hear and respond to the sound of the alarm to wake us out of our complacency and return back to truth, purity, holiness and to the fear of the Lord. We must return back to undivided devotion, and back to that place of pure prayer.

The Bride's invitation is a call to die to self. A call to leave the ways of this world and Babylon behind, all the while being perfected in love, until Christ is completely formed within us. It is an invitation for us to make ourselves ready, by surrendering our will for His in every area of our lives by crucifying our flesh – our needs, wants, ambition, desires, or what we think we need in exchange for His will. It is an invitation to die daily by overcoming sin, adversity, sorrow, loss, rejection, betrayal and fear His way, by becoming the fruit of the Spirit: love, joy, peace, patience, kindness, goodness, faithfulness, humility and self-control [Galatians 4:19, 1 Corinthians 15:31].

The Bride's invitation is a call to intercession. For it is in that deep place of intercessory prayer, where He allows His Bride to touch His lofty heart to bring forth His plans on earth as they exist in heaven. So whatever call is on your life, intercession will be intimately a part of that call. If you are called to be a pastor, teacher, worship leader or missionary – whatever your call; you will be one who lives in that place of prayer in order to fulfill it. Otherwise, it will not happen.

But if we do, it will position us to sit next to Him on His throne, as He Himself overcame and sat next to the Father on His throne. He wants us all to be the Bride of Messiah. He wants us all to rule and reign with Him for all eternity. He wants us all to be freshly prepared wine skins, so He can fill us with His glory. For this is His answer for the dark and turbulent days ahead. If you say, "Yes" to the Bride's invite you will have no regrets. It is worth any price that our Bridegroom King—Yeshua, may ask you to pay! AMEN!

# CHAPTER 2

# OBEDIENCE - BETTER THAN SACRIFICE

*And he who overcomes and who obeys My commands to the [very] end [doing the works that please Me], I will give him authority and power over the nations; and he shall rule them with a sceptre of iron, as when earthen pots are broken in pieces, and [his power over them shall be] like that which I Myself have received from My Father; and I will give him the Morning Star [Revelation 2:26-28 Amp.].*

We see in Revelation 2:26-27 a promise is given to those who overcome, obey His commands and do so until the very end. It is a promise given to the Bride of Messiah. That promise is to rule and reign with the King of kings, during the Millennium Reign, restoring His Kingdom on earth during that 1,000-year period. It is not a promise to everyone in the Body, only to the Overcomers. We see that three things must happen, if we are to be a part of the first resurrection and to rule and reign with Him over the nations. We must overcome life's circumstances, by obeying His commands; and we must endure to the very end [Revelation 20:6].

**JOHN 14:15, 21**
*If you love Me, keep My commandments. He who has My commandments and keeps them, it is he who loves Me.*

*And he who loves Me will be loved by My Father, and I will love him and manifest Myself to him.*

John says, if we love Him, then we will obey Him and He will reveal Himself to us. The Lord longs to reveal Himself to His people, but He needs our obedience to Him to do so.

**How could we define obedience?** It is surrendering power to another by yielding our will to the will of another. Obedience occurs when we change our opinions, judgments or actions because someone in a position of authority told us to do so. A key aspect of obedience is that because we have changed in some way, does not mean that we immediately agree with the change.

How do we know if we are being obedient to Him? 1 John tell us that we ought to walk on this earth in the same manner as He walked.

**1 John 2:3-6**
*Now by this we know that we know Him, if we keep His commandments. He who says, "I know Him," and does not keep His commandments, is a liar, and the truth is not in him. But whoever keeps His word, truly the love of God is perfected in him. By this we know that we are in Him. He who says he abides in Him ought himself also to walk just as He walked.*

We can see from these verses that we will get to know Him only if we obey Him. And, we can obey Him, only if we really love Him. But the more we get to know Him – His ways, thoughts, desires, the more we will want the truth that sets our captive souls free. Obeying Him means we love truth no matter how painful it may be to hear at times. And no matter what it might cost us with time, resources and relationships. The more we obey—love truth, the more the love of God is in our souls. The more our character will become like His in our words, thoughts and deeds.

## Path to Obedience

Pursuing truth in our lives is vital to our obedience; it starts the path to our obedience. Truth leads us into His perfect love, that brings transformation to our souls so we can conduct our lives by the same standards that Yeshua walked while on this earth. It is absolutely possible to overcome our sin nature by the empowerment of the Holy Spirit that was given to us to do so. That is why He gives us grace—His power and strength, so we can overcome and be transformed into His likeness. It was His plan for us from the beginning. It is why He hung on that tree, for us to live and not die, in the fullness of His truth. If we are dying daily to self, our character will become like His more and more with each passing day.

**1 John 2:15-16**
*Do not love the world or the things in the world. If anyone loves the world, the love of the Father is not in him. For all that is in the world—the lust of the flesh, the lust of the eyes, and the pride of life—is not of the Father but is of the world.*

And, if we love Him, we will not love the ways of this world. We will not want to stay in Babylon. We will not want to pursue our carnal desires anymore. We will not live for self, but will pursue 1 Corinthians 13 that tells us that love suffers long and is kind; it does not envy; nor parade itself, is not puffed up; does not behave rudely, or seek its own, it is not provoked, thinks no evil; does not rejoice in iniquity, but rejoices in the truth; bears all things, believes all things, hopes all things, endures all things. We will want to know and become this love that never fails.

**1 John 3:2-3**
*Beloved, now we are children of God; and it has not yet been revealed what we shall be, but we know that when He is revealed, we shall be like Him, for we shall see Him as He is. And everyone who has this hope in Him purifies himself, just as He is pure.*

Our obedience will lead us into purity. We will no longer lust for the world or its ways. Instead, we pursue the One we love wholeheartedly wanting to be purified from our sin – from wrong thought patterns and lifestyle choices, from the stains that Babylon has left upon our souls.

**1 John 3:18-19**
*My little children, let us not love in word or in tongue, but in deed and in truth. And by this we know that we are of the truth, and shall assure our hearts before Him.*

A good indication that we are on the right track to pursuing truth is not only that the world hates us, but that we are becoming more of the fruit of the Spirit: love, joy, peace, patience, kindness, goodness, faithfulness, humility and self-control in our words, thoughts and deeds. We will react and walk after our flesh less, and instead we will respond and walk after the Spirit more frequently. We will have the mind of the Spirit and know life and peace in every situation we face. Our prayer life is affected by how we respond to life's circumstances—for good or for bad, depending on if we react to our flesh or respond and walk after the Spirit.

**1 John 3:21-22 Amp.**
*And we receive from Him whatever we ask, because we [watchfully] obey His orders [observe His suggestions and injunctions, follow His plan for us] and [habitually] practice what is pleasing to Him.*

Our prayers are heard and answered to the degree we have let our souls be purified by the Refiner's fire and to the degree we are willing to obey and become perfected in love. Most Christians pray from their soulish desires, meaning the "Me, I and self." They pray from a materialistic, or selfish gain viewpoint. When they see what they believe is an answer to their soulish prayer, it is really the enemy being allowed to deceive them, because they are not submitted to God's Word and authority in their life, but submitted to Satan's ways. Therefore, they are easily deceived and will remain a carnal, lukewarm Christian, unless they are willing to let go of their low life [Matthew 10:39 Amp.].

> **1 JOHN 4:16-17**
> *And we have known and believed the love that God has for us. God is love, and he who abides in love abides in God, and God in him. Love has been perfected among us in this: that we may have boldness in the day of judgment; **because [that]** as He is, so are we in this world.*

In verse 17 of 1 John 4, where it says, "*...because as He is, so are we in this world.*" The word "because" is not the correct translation. The Greek word is "hoti." It is Strong's G3754.[8] It translates to mean "that" and is used 612 times in the New Testament. This word changes the whole context of what John is saying in this verse. He is saying that as He walked on this earth, we should walk the same as He did. The Lord expects us to do so; we have all been called to be like Him, today. He provided everything that we need to succeed, by giving us the Holy Spirit and abundant grace to conform us into His likeness. May His blood that was spilt for us not be in vain.

## Position of Relationship

John always brings us back to God's love. If we love Him, we will want to obey Him, which means loving truth, purity, and holiness, with our goal to be perfected in love. Our obedience should not be out of a religious to-do list, but from a position of relationship. We love Him, because He first loved us, and not for our selfish gain. Instead, we will love His holy presence and long to dwell within it. We will want to know what He thinks and feels. And when He reveals those desires to us, we will want to conform our lives to His ways. We are to abide in love. When we do, we will stay connected to the Vine and He will abide in us, for this is His promise to us [John 15:4-9].

**JOHN 15:7**
*If you abide in Me, and My words abide in you, you will
ask what you desire, and it shall be done for you.*

When we abide in Him—in love, our prayers will be answered, because they will align with His will for our lives or situations. When we abide in Him, as a lifestyle, we will be able to come before Him boldly on that day of Judgment, when we have to give an account of how we lived our lives on this earth. I believe our first evaluation on that Day will be: *"Did we love Him? Did we obey Him? Did we become love, and especially to the unlovable ones that He allowed into our lives?"*

To get to that place is a process. It is a journey of purification, by the choices we make, and has to be intentional on our part. We will need to appropriate 1 John 1:8-10 in our lives every day. If we think that we have not sinned, we are a liar and the truth is not in us. It is so important that we keep short accounts with the Lord and with one another. We must learn to walk in humility. For He will lead the humble in what is right and teach the humble His ways. We must stay teachable and learn to walk in absolute and explicit obedience. Absolute means: we complete what is asked of us. Explicit means: we followed the instructions to the letter – we did not take short cuts [Psalm 25:9].

**2 CORINTHIANS 7:1**
*Therefore, having these promises, beloved, let us cleanse*

*ourselves from all filthiness of the flesh and spirit,
perfecting holiness in the fear of God.*

The Lord cannot dwell in the unclean and unholy recesses of our hearts. To the degree that we allow Him to purify our souls, He can abide within us. He will not force anyone to go through the process, for He will not go against our will. His desire and perfect will is to be One with us. But very few go that deep in Him because they are not willing to let go of the world, their sin, their lusts, their false belief systems. Very few really obey Him. Therefore, very few really love Him. Too often believers spiritualise His Word and reason it away, thinking that He did not really mean it. We are called to be holy and to obey a holy God. We are called to be prepared vessels for honor, who are useful for the Master to do good work in and through our lives.

**2 TIMOTHY 2:20-21**
*But in a great house there are not only vessels of gold
and silver, but also of wood and clay, some for honor
and some for dishonor. Therefore if anyone cleanses
himself from the latter, he will be a vessel for honor,
sanctified and useful for the Master, prepared for
every good work.*

## Forbidden Sacrifices

In 1 Samuel, the prophet Samuel had given Saul specific instructions after he had anointed him king over Israel. Saul was to wait seven days in Gilgal, until Samuel came to show him how to offer the burnt offerings and the peace offerings. Because Samuel did not come when he expected him to come, the people started to scatter, making Saul fearful of them. He, therefore, offered the burnt offerings and peace offerings without Samuel, which he had been forbidden to do [1 Samuel 10:8, 13:8-9].

As soon as he did, Samuel arrived asking Saul, *"What have you done?"* Saul blamed the people and Samuel for why he did not obey. And because of it, he offered an unholy sacrifice to the Lord. It was a dead work, for this sacrifice could be compared to wood, hay and stubble. It was a big mistake! For Samuel told him that if he had obeyed the commandment of the Lord, that He would have established his kingdom over Israel forever, but now it would be given to another man. Saul suffered a major consequence for his disobedience, but it was not the end of his disobedience [1 Samuel 13:10-14].

In Chapter 15, Samuel instructs Saul to destroy all of the Amalekites – every man, woman, infant, nursing child, ox, sheep, camel and donkey. But he did not do as instructed. Instead, he spared Agag king of the Amalekites, the best sheep, oxen, fatlings, lambs and all that they determined was good. When Samuel went to meet Saul, after Saul failed to complete this holy assignment, he lies to Samuel, telling him that he had obeyed the voice of the Lord. He tries to convince Samuel that it was the people who wanted to take the best of the sheep and oxen and bring them as a sacrifice to the Lord. Samuel then tells him that to obey is better than sacrifice. For rebellion is as the sin of witchcraft, and stubbornness is as iniquity and idolatry, and because he rejected the word of the Lord, the Lord has rejected him from being king [1 Samuel 15:3-23].

The Lord regretted making Saul king, for he did not keep His commands. Saul's disobedience caused him to lie to others, bringing a spirit of deception upon himself, so that he really believed that he obeyed the voice of the Lord. Saul had an obedience issue, which was rooted in the sin of fear of man. And because of it, he did it his way and not the Lord's way [1 Samuel 15:11, 24].

Our disobedience has consequences, where we can suffer loss of our eternal rewards. It does not always end well, or we will get another opportunity to get it right. We see this with Saul. It did not end well for him. He was given more than one opportunity to obey the voice of the Lord. After the kingdom was torn from him and given to David, Saul lost his mind trying to destroy David. Samuel had told him prior that his rebellion was like witchcraft. In Saul's desperation, he seeks a witch for counsel to tell him his future.

Saul was no longer following the Living God. His rebellion brought him into a relationship with a witch, that ultimately caused him to take his own life [1 Samuel 28:7-9, 31:4].

I believe Saul's consequences were severe because he held a powerful and influential position over the people. The Lord loves His people so much that he was not going to let Saul's character flaws and sin cause Him to be mocked. He was not going to let the few destroy the masses with their rebellion and idolatry. And to prove it, He anointed David, a man after His own heart to lead!

Saul's accounting is a serious warning to those who continually refuse to surrender their will and are seeking their own kingdom, and especially to those in leadership. Rebellion has and will cause many to be led into the occult, with some following another "Yeshua," believing they are hearing from God; and especially in these last days, as we see the apostasy increase. We can see that the Lord does not let anyone touch His heart, just because they say they believe in Him. Instead, He qualifies us by the choices we make.

## Realms or Spheres of Authority

We all have different realms or spheres of authority that as a believer, we are to steward. Some of us have more authority than others. How much we have been given depends upon the unique call that is upon our lives and what we need to complete the works that we are to do. For example, we all are given authority over the power of the enemy. As a fallen angel, Satan has no authority over mankind, only power to steal, kill and destroy. But as a believer, we have been given authority and power to destroy Satan's counsel against our lives, communities, cities and nations. And that authority trumps Satan's power, every time!

**LUKE 10:19**
*Behold, I give you the authority to trample on serpents
and scorpions, and over all the power of the enemy, and
nothing shall by any means hurt you.*

**EPHESIANS 2:4-6**
*But God, who is rich in mercy, because of His great love with which He loved us, even when we were dead in trespasses, made us alive together with Christ (by grace you have been saved), and raised us up together, and made us sit together in the heavenly places in Christ Jesus,*

To the degree we obey God's commandments and live a consecrated life unto holiness, will determine how much we walk in the authority and power we have been given. It will also determine how much legal ground we give the enemy to use his power against us, if we choose not to follow the Lamb, wholeheartedly. It is equally important to know our rank and file in the Kingdom of God. When we do, we will function in our divine roles, with each one of us doing our unique part. We will be able to complete the works that we all have to do, individually and corporately, as we make up one Body [1 Corinthians 12:12-27].

**1 CORINTHIANS 12:20-21**
*But now indeed there are many members, yet one body. And the eye cannot say to the hand, "I have no need of you"; nor again the head to the feet, "I have no need of you."*

In 2012, after I had been pursuing a deeper walk and place of intercession with the Lord for several years, the Lord revealed a realm of authority that He had purposed for me to walk into at His appointed time. At the time, I wept, as I could not fathom how or why? At the same time, I understood that unless the Lord gives us authority over certain realms, we would be destroyed if we tried to walk in that authority, without Him giving us the grace to do so. It was not until the call to Ireland came that I could understand better how this authority was going to be necessary in order to do what He was asking of me. We see an example of different levels of authority being given in the parable of the ten minas [Luke 19:11-24].

That same year, the Lord called me to a 40-day fast in preparation of seven days of fasting and prayer that I was to do in Jerusalem. The Lord had given me the dates when I was to leave and when I was to return. He instructed me not to stay with anyone that I knew, but I was to stay in the Old City; and I was to make myself available to Him 24 hours a day. I purposed with all my heart to obey what He was asking. I had no idea why I was to go, or how I would be praying.

Days before I left, the missiles started flying, with many airlines not flying into Israel. Some friends asked if I was still going? I could not fathom not going, for that thought never entered my mind. He was sending me, so I believed He would make a way. And that He did! What I can say about that prayer assignment is that when the Lord told me to make myself available to Him 24 hours a day, I had no idea that He was going to make Himself available to me 24 hours a day. I slept an hour—two at the most each night. I dwelt in the manifest presence of His glory. I became intimately aware of what it meant not to need anything or miss anyone, when in His presence. I left Jerusalem, understanding why it is where His heart beats. I wept and wept, not wanting to leave, for anywhere else was too far away and my heart could not bear it. I offered to stay, but the answer was no, and I was to return to Phoenix. It was only after I obeyed what He asked, did He then reveal Himself, His plans and strategies enabling me to accomplish His eternal purposes for why He sent me for that specific time period.

## Leaders and Followers

Not everyone is called and anointed to lead. Not everyone is anointed to be a general in the Lord's army, but many are to be followers with their own priceless, privileged rank. It does not mean one class is more important than the other, for without each other we will never accomplish God's plans for our lives, communities, cities and nations. It means that God decides the calls, gifts, and the anointings that are upon our lives, because He knows what each of us are capable of accomplishing in order to bring about His eternal plans. It is not a popularity contest, but about our surrender and obedience.

We therefore need to know what our rank is and come into alignment with those plans, and we must do them well. Not just for our own lives, but for those we are to be following. If one is called to lead, and another to follow, and both obey what the Lord is asking, they both will be 100% successful in His eyes and both will bring forth 100% good fruit. That is how He sees and judges our actions.

### JOEL 2:7-8 AMP.

*They run like mighty men; they climb the wall like men of war. They march each one [straight ahead] on his ways, and they do not break their ranks. Neither does one thrust upon another; they walk every one in his path. And they burst through and upon the weapons, yet they are not wounded and do not change their course.*

Too often, many appoint themselves to positions of leadership, operating out of their flesh and building their own kingdoms. It would be advantageous for us to recognise those He has anointed to lead: pastors, teachers, worship leaders, and especially those who have been anointed to lead prayer. It would be advantageous for us to get behind them, instead of finding fault with them. For they can make us feel uncomfortable and not pray in a way that is familiar to us. They can move at a pace and at a depth that we are not used to. Therefore, we can become jealous, critical, competitive, and tear them down. Instead of following, supporting and building God's kingdom with them.

It takes years for God to develop that anointing and call that is on anyone's life in leadership. And especially for those He has chosen to break the yoke that is over a city or nation. These empty vessels desire not to be heard or seen, but they are recognisable because of the power of God that flows from their mouth when they begin to pray. They have no need to write out a script to follow. For they are laid down, 100% surrendered lives, who follow the Lamb wherever He may lead, and particularly in that deep place of intercessory prayer. If there is one thing they do know, they know their abilities come from Him alone and rely solely on His strength and abilities to move in and through them. Their hope, faith, trust and confidence are in Him solely.

### 1 Corinthians 2:2 Amp.

*For I resolved to know nothing (to be acquainted with nothing, to make a display of the knowledge of nothing, and to be conscious of nothing) among you except Jesus Christ (the Messiah) and Him crucified.*

A one-minute or five-minute prayer can be hard for them, as that time is like taking one breath. It is just the beginning, as they tune their spirit to the Holy Spirit's leadings and directives, for they know His voice and leadings intimately. When they pray, time stops as they know it on this earth, and they will take you into the eternal plans of the Father, if you are willing to follow their lead. And not because it has anything to do with who they are, but because of the One Who dwells in the deep reservoirs of their souls and the anointing that the Father placed upon their lives.

We see these two people groups: leaders and followers, in Matthew 21:9, when the Lord made His entrance into Jerusalem riding on a donkey. There were some who went ahead and some who went behind, and all were shouting praises to the King! They were not competing with, or jealous of one another. Their eyes— their focus, was completely on Him and because of it, He was able to bring about His eternal plans and purposes to this earth. He was able to enter the Temple and drive out everything that was profane that was stopping the people from receiving the deliverance and healing they needed. For they were not able to prior, because those who occupied the Temple had made it into a den of robbers and not a house of prayer [Matthew 21:1-14].

## Obedience Precedes a Move of God

Obedience, purity and holiness will always precede a move of God. Without it, it is impossible to know Him and the eternal purposes that He has for us. His Word has conditions. Too often, we gloss this over in the Church. He has conditions to answering our prayers. He is so willing to answer our prayers, but we have our part to do. Most Christians do not understand what it means to obey, or they justify not doing so. They do not understand that prayer requires all of us: spirit, soul and body, if we want to be effective for His Kingdom.

To be obedient has many levels, a depth to it. It is more than a physical act of doing something. It requires that we walk in truth, love, purity and holiness. It is a process of learning from our mistakes, humbling ourselves and yielding our will to His, as often as needed. Our obedience is vital to our prayer life, if we want our prayers not only heard but answered.

We need to learn to dress ourselves in absolute and explicit obedience to the Word of God, that we may be found doing His will, if we want to touch His heart and rule and reign with Him. There truly is nothing more important than to hear and obey the voice of the Lord. Not only the written Word, but the personal instructions that He gives for our lives, families, churches and ministries. He does not want any of us to miss the eternal purposes for why we were created, or to lose the eternal rewards that go with our obedience.

> **JAMES 1:23-25**
> *For if anyone is a hearer of the word and not a doer,*
> *he is like a man observing his natural face in a mirror;*
> *for he observes himself, goes away, and immediately*
> *forgets what kind of man he was. But he who looks into*
> *the perfect law of liberty and continues in it, and is not*
> *a forgetful hearer but a doer of the work, this one will*
> *be blessed in what he does.*

Often, I hear that "fear of intimacy" is what stops many from knowing Him. But the truth is, that the Body does not have an intimacy problem, we have an obedience problem. He disciplines those He loves and that discipline, when it comes into our lives, is meant to bring us back to a right relationship with Him. For it will cause our character to become compatible with His. Obedience is the pathway to an intimate relationship with Him and with the Father [Revelation 3:18-20].

And when we come into that place of intimacy, we will receive the revelation that is needed to know Him and to experience transformation "Zoe Life" in our lives. Equally, that place of intimacy will cause rivers of grace, humility, revelation and understanding to flow, giving us what we need to obey and complete the works we have been sent to do, His way.

There is not always time to make things right; we saw that with Saul. Obedience is vital to touching the heart of God, in order to come before Him with clean hands and a pure heart, so our sacrifices can be acceptable to Him. May we not waste one more second, chasing after emptiness, falseness and futility. Instead, may we ask the Lord to show us every way that we are not obeying Him. May we ask Him for a teachable spirit and the grace to obey. It is a prayer that He will always answer, for He set us up to succeed, not to fail. I once heard a Prophet of the Lord say that when there are not enough words to express our love for Him, obedience says it all! AMEN!

# CHAPTER 3

# THE ROBE OF HUMILITY & MEEKNESS

*Yes, all of you be submissive to one another, and be clothed with humility, for God resists the proud, but gives grace to the humble. Therefore, as the elect of God, holy and beloved, put on tender mercies, kindness, humility, meekness, long suffering; bearing with one another, and forgiving one another, if anyone has a complaint against another; even as Christ forgave you, so you also must do* [1 Peter 5:5, Colossians 3:12-13].

There are three character attributes that we all need, if we are to be conformed into His likeness, and be able to touch the heart of God. We must be obedient, humble and teachable. If we walk in all three, God can do anything with us! But we need all three manifesting in our lives.

Our obedience is the first step to becoming humble. Without it, we will not learn the discipline of clothing ourselves with humility and meekness. If we are not humble, we will not be teachable. We will not be able to receive correction, for our pride will stop us from going into the deeper things of God—to be One with Him.

**PROVERBS 29:1**
*He who is often rebuked, and hardens his neck, will suddenly be destroyed, and that without remedy.*

**JAMES 1:21 AMP.**
*So get rid of all uncleanness and the rampant outgrowth of wickedness, and in a humble spirit receive and welcome the Word which implanted and rooted [in your hearts] contains the power to save your souls.*

**PSALM 25:9 AMP.**
*He leads the humble in what is right, and the humble He teaches His way.*

Yeshua tells us that it is the meek who will inherit the earth. And, it is the faithful servant found doing what the Master wants, who will rule over all His goods and distribute them to those in need. These verses refer to the Overcomers—the Bride of Messiah, who will reign with Him during the Millennium Reign [Psalm 37:11, Matthew 5:5, 24-45-47, Revelation 2:26-27, 20:4-6].

You may say, not so! But let me ask the question, *"When does a person receive an inheritance?"* Is it not always given after a death takes place? If the meek are to "inherit" the earth that means they will do so after they have died. And if after they died, and already in heaven, why would they have any need to be concerned with earthly matters? Because it is a promise to reign with Him and be a part of the first resurrection during the Millennium Reign.

Matthew 24 is all about the last days with the Lord forewarning what is to come and how we should be found when He appears. Verses 45-47 are a promise to the Overcomers to reign with Him. For the Lord tells them right before these verses about the catching away that will take place. If the catching away has taken place, why would these faithful servants have any need to rule over all their master's goods? Because it is a promise to reign with Him during the Millennium Reign.

### Difference Between Humility and Meekness

**ISAIAH 57:15**
*For thus says the High and Lofty One Who inhabits eternity, whose name is Holy: I dwell in the high and*

*holy place, with him who has a contrite and humble spirit, to revive the spirit of the humble, and to revive the heart of the contrite ones*

**How could we define humility?** Lowly, submissive, showing that you do not think of yourself as better than other people, modest.

**How could we define meekness?** Strength under control. For example; a horse runs wild, beautiful to see but not much use to man. On the other hand, when bridled, the horse is useful to man.[9]

Both are character attributes that will cause us to be transformed until Messiah has been formed within our soul. Both greatly affect our relationship with Him and others. And, to the degree that we clothe ourselves with them, these attributes will determine to what degree we fulfill the call that is upon our lives and our destiny. True Kingdom authority is clothed in both attributes.

The more time we spend in prayer, the humbler and meeker we will become by having those intimate conversations with the Lover of our souls. For when we are seeking to know the heart of God, we will find Him. And in His perfect love towards us, He shows us our faults, so that we can become like Him. That intimate fellowship with Him causes scales to fall off our hard hearts, enabling us to see what He sees about ourselves and how we treat others, whether good or bad. When we respond to the Spirit, our pride decreases and His ways increase in our lives.

## Choose Love!

Many years ago, I asked the Lord to teach me the difference between being humble and meek. Both are mentioned in the Word, but I did not know how they differed, but believed they both must be important to Him. So for months I would ask Him to teach me the difference. I knew the very first time that I asked, it was somehow going to be painful. And it was!

About three months before my husband died, the Lord forewarned me, *"That a difficult time was coming and I AM encouraging you to choose love. It will be hard for you, but I AM encouraging you to choose love. It will be your choice."*

When He spoke this word, it put such fear in my heart. For my walk had been about unconditional love – loving the not so lovable, choosing to forgive and die to my expectations of others. And, especially what I ever thought my marriage was going to be like after my husband believed in the Lord. That has always been my choice to this day, no matter what the circumstances. It is not easy and I have failed many times, but there is no other option as far as I am concerned than to pursue love, His way. All grace and more grace!

It is why I was so fearful of what was coming, for it meant it had to be really hard. I went on a 3-day fast with the sole purpose of asking that I would be given the grace, strength and wisdom to be obedient to what He was telling me to do – to choose love, when facing this situation. For I knew my obedience was going to be pivotal in overcoming whatever was coming.

Once I told the Lord my desire to do these 3-days of fasting, He spoke saying, *"Yes, I am giving you what you are asking. For there is more coming and what you have asked for is wise. It pleases me to give you My grace, strength and wisdom to get you through what is coming. I will give you this. Do not take your eyes off Me. Go by what I tell you not by what you see."* I had not ever had that happen before or since, where the Lord answered before I had even started my fast.

It was the toughest 3-day fast, or any fast I have done including the 40-day, 21-day or 7-day fasts to this day. After I broke my fast, the Lord revealed how I thought I was fasting for my immediate situation, but He was doing a deeper work by enlarging my spirit, not just for the present need of what was coming, but laying a spiritual foundation deep within my soul that would be needed for me to fulfill my destiny. It was a shift from the temporal to the eternal, so to speak, and why it was so hard. I have never been the same since walking out those three days with the Lord. I learned about how worthless our ways are to Him and about drinking from the Well of Helplessness, which is a place in Him that was revealed to me.

Initially, I had thought *"to choose love"* had to do with my husband. We had been through so much and I honestly could not imagine what more could be coming. But it had to do with other believers and the words they had spoken to me about my husband the day he died, and how they treated me. Their words were cruel, unjust and caused great sorrow to my heart that was already broken to a billion pieces. The difficult time that I would go through was the death of my husband, a curve ball that I never saw coming.

After a couple of months, while working through my pain towards these believers, He showed me the difference between humility and meekness. I was able to understand the difference, because I had just walked through it, not realising it. As broken as my heart was, I had, weeks prior, stated my case for how they had judged my husband and our life together. I said no more, leaving it to the Lord to protect and defend me. But I kept hearing His words, *"I encourage you to choose love."*

## Painful, Embarrassing and Humiliating!

I knew I had to show love no matter what I was feeling, meaning that I was to stay in relationship and not shut them out, as that is what my flesh wanted to do. It was so hard! There were times where He wanted me to send a card, letting them know I was thinking of them, or make muffins and bring them to their house. My flesh was screaming as the layers came off! But forgiveness is not only a choice, but an action too. When we take that outward step to show love and forgiveness towards those not deserving – not asking for it, it positions Him to do greater works in our lives, where we get promoted on a Kingdom level. And that promotion is often not a material gain, but a spiritual gain to become more like Him.

The Lord taught me that humility is when we humble ourselves before the Lord. And meekness is when we humble ourselves before others. There is nothing too pleasant about learning to be humble and meek. Often it is painful, embarrassing, humiliating and sometimes can feel degrading. Your flesh will die as you take up your cross and follow the Lamb's lead. Both attributes affect our prayer time and are vital to our relationship with Him, for they affect how deep we are allowed to go in Him, just as much as our obedience. Humility and meekness help our faith to grow by giving us the grace that we need to love unconditionally, as He loves us.

In 2017, several years after teaching me this lesson, the Lord spoke this word to me:

*"If we never become humble before Him, we will never become meek before man."*

### The Washing of Our Feet

In John chapter 13:1-12, we see the Lord display great humility and meekness towards His disciples at the Passover Seder, when He took off His outer garments and washed their feet. Peter, initially, did not want Him to wash his feet, until the Lord told him that if He did not, he could not have any part of Him. Yeshua then told them that those who are bathed are already clean and they only need their feet washed. He then gives an odd command, telling them that they were to wash one another's feet and that a servant is not greater than his Master.

What was the Lord teaching them? Humility and meekness before Him and each other. When He said that those who are bathed are clean already and only need their feet washed; He was speaking of salvation. They were already bathed in the blood of the Lamb – they were saved. It is why they did not need to be "bathed" again but only their feet, because a person can only get saved once. Even if a person backslides, they cannot get saved again, they can only repent and turn back to the Lord.

The washing of our feet speaks of our earthly walk with the Lord and with others. It is why only our feet need to be washed. In that walk, our souls get soiled with the cares of this world. We can become offended, prideful, jealous – disobedient to His ways. The Lord washing their feet, speaks of keeping short accounts by coming humbly before Him daily and confessing our faults and our sin to Him. When we do, the blood will wash away our filth. Our walk will stay pure before Him [1John 1:8-9].

The washing of one another's feet speaks of when we are to show someone their fault or sin, in love, with lips full of truth and grace. It is the removal of our outer garment, where we let our undergarments get soiled, in order to bring deliverance and healing to others. It takes great humility and meekness to be able to do that in a way where correction can be heard and received. Equally, it takes great humility and meekness for a person to receive correction. In the natural, most people are uncomfortable having someone else wash their feet. Why? Because most feet are not very pleasant to look at! It is the same with our spiritual washings, but necessary if we are to touch the heart of God.

**JAMES 5:16**
*Confess your trespasses to one another, and pray for one another, that you may be healed. The effective, fervent prayer of a righteous man avails much.*

It is why He gave this example, saying they were to do as He did. Life is all about relationship. He knew there were going to be times that they would take offense with one another, or not walk as they ought and would need to be corrected and bring correction to one another. For our souls are flawed and do not always see where we are stumbling. We need each other to help us find our way out of the darkness. The Lord displayed great humility and meekness when He washed their soiled feet. He took off His outer garments – laying aside His identity, so He could identify with their brokenness and bring the cleansing and refreshment they needed to keep walking with Him and with each other. It is a display of pure, intimate relationship with the Lord and with others.

**MATTHEW 11:29 AMP.**
*Take My yoke upon you and learn of Me, for I am gentle (meek) and humble (lowly) in heart, and you will find rest (relief and ease and refreshment and recreation and blessed quiet) for your souls.*

If our relationships with one another are tainted in any way; if we have aught in our heart – anything negative towards anyone, He cannot receive our sacrifice of prayer. It is why our humility and meekness before Him and each other are vital to becoming the Bride of Messiah and being able to touch His noble heart in that deep place of intercessory prayer.

**MATTHEW 5:23-24**
*Therefore if you bring your gift to the altar, and there remember that your brother has something against you, leave your gift there before the altar, and go your way. First be reconciled to your brother, and then come and offer your gift.*

**MARK 11:25-26**
*And whenever you stand praying, if you have anything against anyone, forgive him, that your Father in heaven may also forgive you your trespasses. But if you do not forgive, neither will your Father in heaven forgive your trespasses.*

Our meekness, or lack of it, affects our relationships either for good or bad. It is important that we can be transparent with one another and learn to communicate with each other kindly and without taking offense, so that we can remain in intimate fellowship with each other. Satan works overtime, wanting us to believe the worst about others, with his goal to divide us. Humbleness and meekness are powerful weapons of warfare that destroy that evil counsel, when we talk with each other in patient, steadfast love and not in judgment.

## Visitation

In 2014, I had a visitation from the Lord, where He came and placed upon me a cape-like garment around my shoulders. This garment was not attractive. It was drab in color, a dull brown, a bit frumpy, and rough in texture, like burlap. Its length was to my elbows and it fastened around my neck. Although it was not much to look at, I really loved it! And it fit me perfectly. He then spoke to me about the Robe of Humility:

*"Daughter, I have placed upon you My Robe of Humility. I will teach you My ways so that you can understand Me and know Me so you can fulfill your destiny. It is painful to be rejected, to be loved or liked one day and disposed of the next day. This is the heart of man that has not chosen My ways. This is the heart of man whose mind has not been renewed. These painful lessons are for your good to enable you to endure. Although you have tasted and walked through much sorrow, affliction and rejection. There is a different sorrow that comes when it is from those who say they love Me, or know Me. Your tears have comforted Me. Many hearts are only going to grow colder in the days to come. There are few vessels who will yield to this suffering. It is not easy teaching others. It cannot be done in one's own strength and not all, actually very few are called to be teachers, for some of the very reasons you have witnessed these past few weeks that has caused you great sorrow. Too many teach from their souls. They do not know Me and create more problems for those earnestly wanting truth. I AM the One Who called you and chose you in the furnace of affliction. Few are willing to teach My Word in purity, in holiness, without compromise. I will not fail you. Do not be anxious, do not compare yourselves to others. Keep your eyes on Me. Stay low and broken before Me. Fear not man, but the One who can destroy both the body and the soul. The laborers are few and the harvest is ready. We are in a battle for souls. The warfare*

*will be intense, but I will equip My Bride with everything she needs to fight this battle with Me. All that I have is hers and she is all Mine. Many have been called to be My Bride – very few, sadly, will be chosen. This brings great sadness to My heart, but great joy to those who have considered Me worthy, worth knowing. Who have and are willing to pay any price to be One with Me. You will often feel abandoned [by others] in doing My work – are you willing? "Yes Lord." Know in your abandonment by man, I will be with you always."*

## The Robe of Humility

Later that same evening, after a time of worship, I was thanking the Lord for this garment, telling Him how it was the most beautiful garment, robe that He could ever give me. I told the Lord that I did not care what others may think of it, and how much I loved it. I marveled at how it fit me perfectly. I treasured it and wanted to wear it everywhere with everything! Thinking how it was the highest honor to be able to wear this robe—despite what anyone may think of how it looks. It was the most beautiful garment that I could have ever been given, not believing that I was truly worthy to wear it. As I was marveling at the "gift" that had been given to me, the Lord continued to speak about the Robe of Humility, saying:

*"Very few earn the right, the privilege to wear this Robe. There is a high price to be paid for it and few are willing to pay that price. Many tell Me they want My humility but when I bring circumstances into their lives to allow them to walk in My humility, they do not want it, they want their pride, they do not want to humble themselves before others, they are not willing to be corrected. When someone asks Me for humility, it is not automatic. It has to be earned through trials and circumstances; it is the only way to receive it. You have asked Me for years to "clothe you in layers and layers of My Robes of humility and meekness." Today I put My Robe of Humility around you.*

*You did not really understand what that looked like when you have asked this of Me, but you knew it was necessary. And through the different circumstances in your life, you have 'earned' this Robe. Most think it is something I will do for them, that it will automatically happen, but that is not so. They have to choose to walk in humility and as they prove to be faithful in this, they earn the right to wear this Robe. You have paid a high price to wear this Robe. You are baffled, you never saw it this way until now. It starts with a heart that asks Me for humility but at that time it is not granted; what is granted is to bring that person through situations that will bring them to the place of being able to wear this Robe. They will decide in the choices they make. You are remembering when I came to you over five years ago after asking you to come be My Bride, when I visited you a week later and I gave you the first key. I had told you it was the Key of Humility and that you must learn to walk in it or it is impossible to do My works, impossible for you to do what I have called you to do. You have never forgotten that and have been faithful to ask Me to help you be humble, to be meek, to surrender your will for Mine all these years. This Robe will give you the grace you need to overcome in the past where you felt you had failed, and the grace you need to overcome harder testings to stay humble and meek."*

**ISAIAH 66:2**
*For all those things My hand has made, and all those things exist, says the Lord. But on this one will I look: On him who is poor and of a contrite spirit, and who trembles at My word.*

## God is Attracted to the Meek

God is attracted to the meek and works His eternal purposes through them. He loves to use small things to accomplish His great purposes. Being meek causes the favor of the Lord to come upon our lives. May we not misunderstand what it means to have God's favor. Mary, Abel, Noah, were all were favored by the Lord. Lot was favored and escaped the wrath of God, but lost most things dear to him. Joseph was favored, yet his brothers sold him into slavery and he spent 22 years in prison. When God's favor comes, it births something new in our lives, where nothing is ever the same again. We see that in the lives of those mentioned.

God's favor means difficulty, hardship, pressure, persecution, betrayal, rejection, pain, trials and tribulation. Paul taught that it was with much hardship and tribulation that one must enter the Kingdom of God [Acts 14:22]. Most teach or believe in the Church that God's favor means: being prosperous, nice house, cars, money in their bank account. That is not favor from God, but God's blessings, for all things come from Him.

God's favor in our lives means that at some point everything changes, and it will never be the same again. God rocks our world and everything gets flipped upside down. The course of our lives changes drastically, with one purpose—wanting to birth His eternal plans in and through us. And while we are learning to die to self, He is restoring us back to that place of intimate fellowship that Adam and Eve had with Him in the Garden before the fall, who were filled with His glory and clothed in His Light. For that is His plan for those willing to walk in purity, humility and meekness before a holy God and with each other.

## Empty Water Pots

We see in Yeshua' first miracle, turning the water into wine, at the wedding in Cana of Galilee how He revealed our Father's eternal purposes for mankind by declaring the end from the beginning. Galilee in Hebrew means "revealing." Everything Yeshua does is with eternal purpose. It was on the third day that a wedding took place. He was letting everyone know, from the very first miracle, how it is going to end. That a transfiguration and a Wedding is going to take place in vessels who had made themselves ready [John 2:1-11, Isaiah 46:10, Revelation 19:7-9].

At the wedding in Cana, the Lord used empty water pots to turn water into wine to reveal to mankind what He is going to do in those who are empty of themselves. There were six stone water pots, which represents mankind, as six is the number for man. They were stone and not clay. It was because stone was pure, it could not become unclean. Clay could become impure and had to be destroyed. These pots were set apart for one purpose only—for purification. This speaks of our undivided devotion and consecration to be holy, as He is holy. Yeshua chose vessels that were empty. This speaks of our call to die to self daily, until it is no longer I who live, but Messiah who lives in me. He then filled these empty vessels to the brim. This speaks of the indwelling of the Seven Spirits of the Lord and the transfiguration that will take place in those vessels who are set apart for His purposes.

We see that Yeshua poured clean water only into empty vessels who were set apart, pure – no mixture, and used them to manifest His glory, revealing His eternal plans for mankind. He saved the best wine for last; those who will be the Bride of Messiah. But He cannot pour old wine into new wine skins. Likewise, He cannot fill us with His glory, if we are not prepared for it. Meaning, our souls purified in our words, thoughts and deeds. If He did, it would destroy us.

The empty water pots were simple in design. They were modest and lowly. They served their function and did it without compromise. For those who will become like those water pots, He will fill to the brim with the Seven Spirits of the Lord; the same power that raised Him from the dead. He will entrust them to rule over the nations with a rod of iron during the Millennium Reign, because they have clothed themselves in the nature of the Lamb – utterly humble and meek before God and before man. For true Kingdom authority walks clothed in humility and meekness. It is not about self, but all about His will being done, and the needs of others above their own.

## Embrace Your Trials

It takes great grace and humility to become like those pure water pots. We must learn to embrace our trials, for this earth is our training ground, all training us to reign with Him. We have to be intentional in the choices we make and how we spend our time, every day. We need to ask Him to teach us to be humble and meek. And to give us the grace, courage, humility and obedience—whatever we need, to walk in it in our relationships that we may become like Him. It will be painful, but I promise it will be worth it!

If you do, the Robe of Humility will come upon your life, enabling you to stand in His holy place. For His Bride cannot stand in His holy place without being clothed in this garment. This garment will not be attractive to your flesh. It will not compliment you and tell you everything is okay, when it is not. It will not be made of the finest fabric and make you feel comfortable. Instead, it will be rough against your skin causing your flesh to die to your needs, wants and ambitions. It will not be comfortable to wear, but may you buy this garment at whatever price it may cost you! For it will not be possible to touch the heart of God without it. AMEN!

# RENEWAL OF THE MIND

*I beseech you therefore, brethren, by the mercies of God, that you present your bodies a living sacrifice, holy, acceptable to God, which is your reasonable service. And do not be conformed to this world, but be transformed by the renewing of your mind, that you may prove what is that good and acceptable and perfect will of God* [Romans 12:1-2].

God has a dream—did you know that? The Father wants His family restored back to that same place of intimate fellowship that Adam and Eve experienced in the Garden, in the cool of the day, before the fall of man. Family can mean a lot of different things to us, depending on how we were brought up and what our experiences have been. Family can mean: a mom, a dad, grandparents, maybe you were adopted, siblings, fond memories of family gatherings and holidays. Or, often, for many people, it means pain—a lot of unresolved pain. For many of us come from backgrounds, riddled with wounds that were caused from our broken relationships that we had while growing up.

Families are of "like" seed, as they have the same DNA as other family members. At birth, we become that "seed" that is unique to our family's lineage and attributes. As we grow up, we produce the fruit of that seed. It can be good, bad or a combination. Our earthly families and what we experienced growing up affects our relationship with the Lord on the deepest of levels. At our new birth, His Seed is planted into our spirit man. It is the most excellent Seed that is able to heal and transform us, but it is a process for it to grow and to bear good fruit in our lives.

When our wounds are not healed God's way, we bring the damage they have done into every one of our relationships, whether we realise it or not, causing more bad seeds to be sown. Some of those seeds sprout quickly. Others lie dormant for a long time, making us think they no longer have a stronghold over our emotions, thought life or how we treat ourselves and others, wrongly.

## Flowers Versus Weeds

To help illustrate, let me say it this way. Every one of us is created in His image. Therefore, at birth, we are all meant to be beautiful flowers. But until we accept the Lord into our lives, our flower cannot grow and blossom. Instead, we are growing up as a weed without any hope of true everlasting, life-giving, transformation in our lives. As a believer, we need His Spirit within our soul to uproot the offshoots of what those bad seeds had produced in our lives, which is a lot of weeds, in order to experience transformation "Zoe Life."

The renewal of our mind is vital for this process to take place. Without the renewal of our minds taking place, we are like a flower in a garden that needs a good weeding. Have you ever seen how a weed takes over a plant and wraps itself around it, causing it to be bent over? It is the same for us; we become bent over—spiritually and emotionally, with the weeds of our past wrapped around our minds and emotions, keeping us in bondage and stealing the life-giving nutrients that are needed to nourish our souls – the truth that will set them free.

Yeshua teaches about the soil of our hearts in the parable of the seeds in Luke, Chapter 8. Some of the seed fell by the wayside and was trampled. Some fell on rock but died without water. Some fell on thorns, sprang up but was choked to death. And some fell on good soil and produced 100% good fruit. The Seed that Yeshua is talking about is the Word of God. And He wants us to know that to the degree that we embrace it, will determine the outcome of our lives. He is talking about embracing truth, which can often be hard for the unrenewed mind to hear [Luke 8:5-15].

> **How could we define embrace?** If you embrace a change, political system, or idea, you accept it and start supporting it or believing in it.[10]

One of those truths that is hard for a believer to embrace, is that unless our lives become like a grain a wheat that falls into the ground and dies, we will not bear much fruit.

> **JOHN 12:24**
> *Most assuredly, I say to you, unless a grain of wheat falls into the ground and dies, it remains alone; but if it dies, it produces much grain.*

> **1 CORINTHIANS 15:36 AMP.**
> *You foolish man! Every time you plant seed, you sow something that does not come to life [germinating, springing up, and growing] unless it dies first.*

Like a seed, our wills must fall to the ground and die. If not, we will not bear much fruit. We must die to self to produce good spiritual and physical fruit. At our new birth, literally a death took place, our old man died inside. We were given His Seed, the new man on the inside, but we still have the old man on the outside, our flesh that needs to die—to be crucified [Colossian 3:5, Galatians 5:19-21].

> **ROMANS 6:3-6**
> *Or do you not know that as many of us as were baptized into Christ Jesus were baptized into His death?[4] Therefore we **were buried with Him through baptism into death,** that just as Christ was raised from the dead by the glory of the Father, even **so we also should***

*walk in newness of life. For if we have been united together in the likeness of His death, certainly we also shall be in the likeness of His resurrection, knowing this, that our old man was crucified with Him, that the body of sin might be done away with, that we should no longer be slaves of sin.*

When we embrace truth, we embrace the power of the Cross. And when we do, the same power that raised Yeshua from the dead will flow through us, transforming us into His likeness, into newness of life. For when we crucify and bury our flesh with the same baptism of death that the Lord experienced, it will cause us to experience His resurrection power.

The Lord wants intimate fellowship with us and for us to have intimate fellowship with each other. He wants us to be free from sin and bondage that is separating us from Him and from others. But how do we get there when we have a lot of pain, wounds, character flaws, emotional and physical bondage to overcome? The renewal of our mind is vital to our transformation.

**EPHESIANS 4:23 AMP.**
*And be constantly renewed in the spirit of your mind [having a fresh mental and spiritual attitude],*

## The Battle for Our Soul

Paul tells us that it is our flesh that wars against our spirit man. This is where we stumble over and over in our walk by doing the very things we hate doing. Until our minds are renewed in those areas of our lives that are wounded, we will continue to stumble. It is the old man on the outside – our flesh, that is warring against the new man on the inside. It can feel at times like a constant battle. And because the battle is great, it is why so little transformation takes place in a believer's life, for many give into their fleshly desires. For the call to our flesh to surrender our will for His will,

will not concede without a fight. It is why so many in the Church are still a slave to their sin and bondage, for they struggle to surrender their will. But this is the battle that all believers face, and we are all called to overcome with the grace He has given us to do so.

**GALATIANS 5:17**
*For the flesh lusts against the Spirit, and the Spirit against the flesh; and these are contrary to one another, so that you do not do the things that you wish.*

So, how do we overcome? In order to do so, we have to understand what is taking place on the inside of us. We have to understand the inter-relational struggle that is going on with our spirit, soul and body [flesh], and how it is our soul or mind that needs to be renewed. If not renewed, we will see others, circumstances and self through a cloudy lens—the filter of our soul's wounds, when going through trials or in day-to-day circumstances. When we do, we have a 'perceived reality' that becomes our reality but not what is true reality.

## Our Soul is Our Mind

Our soul is our mind. It is where we make decisions. It is our intellect, the seat of our emotions, where our history is stored: life's events – both good and bad, thoughts, emotions, childhood trauma, unhealed wounds, generational iniquities that have not been dealt with, along with all the horrible things that have happened to us in life. Like a hard drive, it constantly takes in and stores data. As our mind gets renewed, a lot of "bad files" get deleted and replaced with good files!

We all have wounds and the effects that sin brought into our lives that need to be healed, cleansed and restored. If not, those wounds or the residual effects of our sin life will distort what is true and affect our relationships in a negative way. Or, at best case, we will remain stagnant and not mature and accomplish God's plans for our lives.

For example, when a child is not wanted when conceived, a wound of rejection is put upon its soul in the mother's womb. They will grow up thinking that no one likes them, and that others are purposely excluding them. They become withdrawn and often live in self-pity because they filter relationships through what becomes a 'perceived hurt' on their end in their current relationships. They take offense and believe the lies the enemy has whispered into their ears. They do not believe the good report about others or themselves. Therefore, they cannot see what is praiseworthy in their lives and situations around them.

Another example is when a child grows up in an abusive relationship. He or she will grow up to be a very angry, rageful, resentful, bitter adult. Some will display that anger in a passive aggressive way. It gets directed at the very ones who should have protected them, but did not. They have a hard time with authority and submitting to it. The walls are so high, it is hard for anyone to reach them. They will go to great lengths to protect themselves. If not fully healed, that anger and bitterness seeps into every relationship, leaving a trail of destruction behind.

When our mind is not renewed and we face adversity, it triggers those wounds – those ungodly desires, and sends a message to our body or flesh, telling it to react in a way that does not align with the Word. We will walk after our flesh and not after the Spirit, over and over again.

**Spirit =** Our new man
**Soul =** Our mind, emotions
**Body =** Our flesh

We have two voices that tell our flesh or body what to do: our spirit or our soul. When our mind is not renewed in the area of our life that needs to be refined with fire, then our soul partners with our weak flesh and we do the very things we hate. But if the two voices: spirit and soul, join together, our spirit man will dominate our flesh and tell it what to do. It will resist the devil and cause him to flee. That is called crucifying the flesh. When we do, we are walking after the Spirit and no longer being a slave to our flesh's ungodly desires and unholy appetites.

**GALATIANS 2:20**
*I have been crucified with Christ; it is no longer I who live, but Christ lives in me; and the life which I now live in the flesh I live by faith in the Son of God, who loved me and gave Himself for me.*

Most times, believers walk after their flesh, where their soul and flesh are joined together warring against their spirit man. Most decisions they make are from their soul—an unrenewed mind, therefore they are not in the will of God. If our spirit man is to grow and mature and dominate our flesh, then a death to our flesh must take place. It is easier said than done, but we must do it as often as needed, leaning on the power of the Holy Spirit and the grace we have been given, until our spirit and soul have 'killed' our flesh and buried it once and for all!

**ROMANS 8:6-8**
*For to be carnally minded is death, but to be spiritually minded is life and peace. Because the carnal mind is enmity against God; for it is not subject to the law of God, nor indeed can be. So then, those who are in the flesh cannot please God.*

When we walk in the flesh, meaning, when we choose not to crucify it, by exchanging our will for His will, we are an enemy to God. We cannot please Him. We are not growing in Him. It is why our souls need to be saved, by the renewal of our minds. When we do, we are restored back to the truth that will set us free. Every believer should be on this journey – daily – living the crucified life, saying, *"Not my will be done, but His will be done."* Paul said, I die daily. For when we do, we will know the power of His resurrection life flowing into our souls.

**PHILIPPIANS 3:10-11**
*that I may know Him and the power of His resurrection, and the fellowship of His sufferings, being conformed to His death, if, by any means, I may attain to the resurrection from the dead.*

## Resist the Devil and He Must Flee!

In Kenneth E. Hagin's book, *I Believe in Visions*, he shared how the Lord came and taught him how demons are able to influence Christians minds if allowed to do so. The Lord told him that as long as the Christian rejects the evil spirit—sinful thought, it flees. But if they entertain the evil thought, it becomes a black spot on their minds and they become obsessed with the evil spirit's wicked desire. At that point, the believer can still resist the demon and it would have to flee.

But if they do not, that black dot moves from their mind into their heart and then it is too late. That thought will manifest as sin in their life and there is nothing anyone can do to cast it out, because they want it, and He will not go against our wills. In this case, it was a pastor's wife who became disillusioned with her husband's ministry and believed the lie that she had wasted her life. She soon entered into an adulterous relationship, leaving her husband. She eventually lost her salvation. It was not because she had committed adultery, the Lord would have forgiven her, if she had asked, but it was because that sin led her to turn her back completely on the Lord.[11]

**2 CORINTHIANS 2 10:4-6**
*For the weapons of our warfare are not carnal but mighty in God for pulling down strongholds, casting down arguments and every high thing that exalts itself against the knowledge of God, bringing every thought into captivity to the obedience of Christ, and being ready to punish all disobedience when your obedience is fulfilled.*

Paul says that we are to pull down strongholds, cast down arguments and every high thing that exalts itself against the knowledge of God. When we do, we are staying engaged in the battle that rages against our mind, by punishing all disobedience, when we obey His Word and plans for our lives. At the same time, we must filter our thought life through Philippians 4:8.

**PHILIPPIANS 4:8**
*Finally, brethren, whatever things are **true**, whatever things are **noble**, whatever things are **just**, whatever things are **pure**, whatever things are **lovely**, whatever things are of **good report**, if there is any **virtue** and if there is anything **praiseworthy—meditate on these things.***

As the shakings increase in these last days, we are going to have ample opportunities to take offense with others and be fearful of what are eyes will see. But we cannot afford to do so, if we are to finish our race, and finish it well! Philippians 4:8 is about the renewal of our mind, by filtering every thought that enters through what is truth. It is a narrow filter that we are to strive to enter our thoughts through, if we want to have the mind of the Spirit and have life and peace in the situations we will face.

**How could we define true?** Conforming to reality or fact, not false or wrong, free from error, authentic – not imagined.

**How could we define noble?** Having high moral qualities, ideals or character, a moral or mental [mind] character of excellence.

**How could we define just?** Free from favoritism, self-interest, bias or deception, guided by truth – what is morally right and fair.

**How could we define pure?** Freedom from foreign or inappropriate elements, anything that contaminates, pollutes, any admixture or modifying addition. Freedom from sin, guilt or evil; it is innocence, chastity, cleanness, without moral defects.

**How could we define lovely?** Having a beauty that appeals to the heart as well as to the eye. Morally, spiritually attractive, gracious.

**How could we define good report?** A true story about somebody doing something good.

**How could we define virtue?** Moral excellence, thinking and doing what is right and avoiding what is wrong.

**How could we define praiseworthy?** Deserving of approval and admiration.

## Be Anxious for Nothing

Paul says that when we do this, the God of peace will be with us – no matter what we are facing. In Philippians 4:6 we are told to be anxious for nothing, instead pray with thanksgiving and that when we do, the peace of God that passes all understanding will guard our hearts and minds. When we pray with a thankful heart, it guards our hearts and minds. Isaiah 26:3 says that the Lord will keep us in perfect peace when our mind is stayed on Him, because our trust is in Him.

Paul learned that in whatever state he was in, to be content. He knew want, he knew gain and he knew persecution. He knew intimately the resurrection power of the Cross, for he died daily, to his desires. He learned that he could do all things through Messiah, Who strengthened him. Paul knew His God intimately and that He would liberally supply his every need according to His riches in glory in Messiah Yeshua. Paul knew how to lean on the Lord's strength, wisdom and counsel, and how to abide in love; loving his enemies and praying for those who persecuted him.

If we want peace, as the shakings continue, we must abide in His love. What does it mean to abide? It means: to stay, to remain. In other words, stay faithful to Him, to His Word, to the call on our lives and to be molded into His likeness no matter how hard it feels at times. It means we are not to lean upon our weaknesses – our weak flesh, but to lean upon His grace and strength—His power to perfect His love into our souls that need to be restored, all the while healing our wounds.

When our minds are renewed in the Spirit of our mind, we learn to live a lifestyle of abiding in love, which is vital for us to overcome these last days that are upon us, His way. For becoming love is our protection for the turbulent days ahead. Psalm 91:1 says, *"He who dwells in the secret place of the Most High will remain stable under the shadow of His wings."* The "secret place" is that place of abiding in His love. For that is what the Lord told me, years ago, while seeking to know where I could find it. So, we could say, *"He who dwells 'in love' will remain stable under the shadow of His wings"* [AP]. How much we are divinely protected is conditional on how much we abide in love. When we pull down strongholds, cast down arguments and filter our thought-life through Philippians 4:8 we will be able to love Him with all of our heart, soul, mind and strength.

**MARK 12:30**
*And you shall love the Lord your God with all your heart, with all your soul, with all your mind, and with all your strength. This is the first commandment.*

When we do, we will have the peace that passes all understanding, when we see life expiring all around us. For war is coming—persecution is coming. But the Lord does not want us to be fearful. Instead, He wants us to be prepared for what is coming. And there is only one way to be prepared: by overcoming by the blood of the Lamb, by the word of our testimony and by not loving our lives, unto death, in every situation we are facing now, that we may be counted worthy to stand before the Son of Man [Luke 21:36].

## One Choice at a Time

When we understand what is happening on the inside of us, we can recognise the battle and make choices that align with the Word. Often, it is one choice at a time, every day, with everything that we go through. And if we are intentional about it, it gets easier. It takes time and it cannot happen overnight. But the Lord in His faithfulness, will orchestrate situations that will expose the tares in our souls that need to be uprooted, by bringing them to the surface. He will always do so when He knows that we are able to deal with them His way, and when we can bear good fruit.

When our flesh dies, our mind or soul becomes renewed, and we experience resurrection power, transforming us to be like Yeshua in that area we have crucified. For a death takes place, where the old man on the outside is being crucified. Transformation comes to our soul and our spirit man grows. This is what changes us from one degree of glory to the next. For His Light comes and takes over that area in our soul that was dark, causing us to be more like Yeshua in word, thought and deed. When we die daily, we are like seed that keeps falling to the ground, that bears fruit, causing newness of life to come forth!

Every day we face a multitude of decisions. We face adversity; we encounter people that rub us the wrong way. That is life. In those moments, are we making decisions that align with God's Word? Or, doing it the world's way? Are we choosing not to retaliate, or harbor feelings of bitterness or unforgiveness? Are we choosing to abide in love? When we do, we become a living sacrifice. And every time, the resurrection power of the Cross enters into us, transforming and enabling us to overcome sin and take our thoughts captive. When our flesh is crucified, our soul is restored and healed in an area that was hurting us. For that to take place, we will need to die to what we think are our needs and our worldly desires.

## Embracing the Cross

At our new birth, the Father imprinted in our spirit the purpose for our life. If we are not willing to become that seed that falls to the ground and dies, so that newness of life can come forth, we will never fulfill the purpose for our lives. If we do not know our purpose, our walk will be aimless and incomplete. We will look to the things of this world—the temporal, where we will never be satisfied. Our first purpose as a believer is to be conformed to the image of Messiah. Many quote Romans 8:28, which tells us that all things are working together for our good who love God and are called according to His purpose. But few quote verse 29 that tells us those difficulties are meant to conform us into His likeness. For He predestined every believer to live the crucified life.

> **ROMANS 8:28-29**
> *And we know that all things work together for good to those who love God, to those who are the called according to His purpose. For whom He foreknew, He also predestined to be conformed to the image of His Son, that He might be the firstborn among many brethren.*

When we do not embrace the crucified life, we do not embrace the Cross. When we do not embrace the Cross, we do not embrace our purpose for life. When we do not embrace our purpose for life, we will never be satisfied and will embrace something else. Those other things may satisfy us temporarily, the unrenewed part of our souls, but will bring us spiritual death, and we will miss our eternal purpose.

When we embrace truth, we die and make an altar. We feel the death, for it hurts when our flesh burns on that altar of sacrifice. But something new takes place on the inside, and how we once reacted, God begins to melt it out of us. We start changing. His resurrection power is released on the inside of us, and we respond to circumstances in a way that will surprise us. That is the process. It will work the fruit of the Spirit into our souls. We will become compatible with His character and Satan will no longer have a hold over our lives. We will understand, intimately, that all things really are working together for our good, especially in what seems like our failures.

It is His way to restore us back to intimate fellowship, where we depend upon Him completely. He is a good Father, His ways are perfect. The Father wants His family to be restored back to pure, intimate fellowship with Him. He wants us to grow into mature sons of God. Ultimately, the Father is after a Bride for His Son, who will be equally yoked to Him in word, thought and deed.

Understanding the conflict within and the renewal of our minds are vital, if we are to grow and mature. He wants to restore all things in our lives, but we have a lot to say about that by the choices we make. It is all by grace—His power and ability to do it in us and through us. It is nothing that we can do in our own strength. He just needs a heart that will say, "Yes" to His ways. A heart that is willing to exchange its will for His, wholeheartedly.

## Testimony of His Character

He wants us to be a testimony of His name—a testimony of His character: true, noble, just, pure, lovely, of good report, virtue, praiseworthy – deserving of approval and admiration, where we display the fruit of the Spirit. He wants us to be a testimony of His love; those who will love truth and obey His Word, no matter what the cost. He wants us to be a testimony of His mercy, where we will love our enemies and pray for those who persecute us—always, and in all circumstances. He wants us to be a testimony of His miracle working powers, where we will do greater works than He did, so that the Lamb may be magnified and glorified through our lives.

In order to do so, we must constantly be renewed in the spirit of our mind and learn a lifestyle of abiding in love. When we do, our soul will be transformed, enabling us to touch the heart of God. For without that transformation taking place, we cannot know Him, nor will our character match His in our words, thoughts and deeds.

## The Door of Your Heart

Can you hear Yeshua knocking on the door of your heart? Will you open and let Him expose the tares that need to be uprooted? Are you willing to do it His way, or do you want to keep doing it your way that has failed, time after time? Are you willing to truly surrender your will for His? If you answered, "Yes," please know that it will be humbling and painful. You will experience disappointments, rejection and betrayal and be misunderstood and judged harshly, at times. But the affliction will seem as if a moment, compared to the transformation it will bring to your soul, all qualifying you to rule and reign with Him for all of eternity, as the Lamb's wife. AMEN!

# HOLINESS – SANCTIFIED & SET APART

*Therefore do not be ashamed of the testimony of our Lord, nor of me His prisoner, but share with me in the sufferings for the gospel according to the power of God, who has saved us and called us with a holy calling, not according to our works, but according to His own purpose and grace which was given to us in Christ Jesus before time began* [2 Timothy 1:8-9].

When we go through sufferings, His way, not only do they become redemptive in recovering the eternal purpose for our lives, but they cause the fragrance of holiness to permeate us, bringing the manifested presence of God into our spheres of influence. Few in the Body today take their holy call seriously. Most do not know what it means to be holy, let alone display it. Holiness is not automatic in our lives. Most believe they are made holy because they believe in Yeshua. But that is not scriptural and not what the Lord teaches through His Word.

**1 PETER 1:13-16**
*Therefore gird up the loins of your mind, be sober, and rest your hope fully upon the grace that is to be brought*

*to you at the revelation of Jesus Christ; as obedient children, not conforming yourselves to the former lusts, as in your ignorance; but as He who called you is holy,* **you also be holy in all your conduct,** *because it is written, Be holy, for I am holy.*

**HEBREWS 12:14**
*Pursue peace with all people, and holiness, without which no one will see the Lord:*

Holiness is not an ideology—a system of ideas or ideals. It is a state of being. It is not passive, instead it is active. Holiness demands that we love the Lord with all of our heart, soul, mind and strength, which can only be done when we are constantly being renewed in the spirit of our mind. When we do, we will worship Him in the beauty of holiness [Mark 12:30, 1 Chronicles 16:29].

**1 CHRONICLES 16:29**
*Give to the Lord the glory due His name; Bring an offering, and come before Him. Oh, worship the Lord in the beauty of holiness!*

**How could we define holiness?** It is a state of being set apart from ordinary purposes. A life of total devotion to God.

Holiness is a state of constant change in one's life – spiritually, physically, emotionally and financially. It is a state of being, in which we choose to reject everything that is unclean, impure and profane in our words, thoughts and deeds. It is a choice to be consecrated— set apart from this world's worthless ways of doing things. Without holiness, no one will see the Lord. We are commanded to pursue holiness in all of our conduct and to be holy, as the Lord is holy [Hebrews 12:14, 1 Peter 1:15-16].

Israel was called to holiness. Instead, they pursued their idols and went after emptiness, falseness and futility, and they became worthless and fruitless to the Lord. When holiness is forged into our character, we will no longer pursue the lusts of our flesh or this world anymore. We will become vessels of noble use, who will produce abundant, good fruit [Jeremiah 2:3-5 Amp., John 10:10].

The pursuit of truth, purity, humility, obedience and the fear of God are all required if our conduct on this earth is to be holy. Years ago, Bobby Conner shared how the Lord told him that anything the Lord did not initiate in his life, it was vile to Him. So anything that we have initiated, no matter how good it may seem, we must know that those works are vile to Him. They are not holy to Him. Instead, they are worthless and fruitless to His Kingdom with no eternal value and will burn up on that Day of Judgment as wood, hay and stubble.

## Nadab and Abihu

We see this with Nadab and Abihu, who were Aaron's sons, whose lineage was the Levitical priesthood. They entered the Temple and offered profane fire – unholy incense, which the Lord had not commanded them. Their motives were impure. They had been drinking before they made their offering. And because of it, His holiness consumed them with a holy fire and they died prematurely [Leviticus 10:1-3, 8-10].

He is a holy God, Who is the same yesterday, today and forever. He changes not. His holiness demands that we come before Him in purity. Today, many in the Church would be like Nadab and Abihu—burnt ashes, from all the unholy offerings they are bringing into His Sanctuary. The dispensation of grace that came with Yeshua's death and resurrection is the only reason many have not suffered the same premature death as Nadab and Abihu. Yeshua made a way for us to enter the Holy of Holies, without being destroyed because of His righteousness—blessed be His name forever, but He did not change what is required for us to touch the heart of God.

**MATTHEW 5:23-24**

*Therefore if you bring your gift to the altar, and there remember that your brother has something against you, leave your gift there before the altar, and go your way. First be reconciled to your brother, and then come and offer your gift.*

**MATTHEW 5:25**

*Agree with your adversary quickly, while you are on the way with him, lest your adversary deliver you to the judge, the judge hand you over to the officer, and you be thrown into prison.*

We are told that if we have anything in our hearts against anyone, we are to leave are offering and go and make amends, before we come before Him. And we are to quickly come to terms with our accusers. Meaning, we need to work out our differences with one another quickly. For if we do not, the Judge will bring His sentence upon our lives. It does not mean His fire is going to destroy us. It means our prayers will not be heard. If we are to touch the heart of God, we must learn to walk in unoffended love. We must become that holy love that is unoffendable, for as the gross darkness increases, we are going to have many opportunities to become offended. Walking in holy love does not mean that we agree or ignore with what is false and evil. Instead, we must respond to it in truth, purity, holiness and in the fear of the Lord. We are to be a light in that place of darkness.

As we see the apostasy increase, we will see an increase of grumblers, complainers, who walk according to their own lusts, mouthing great swelling words, flattering people to gain advantage. We will see mockers in these last days who will walk according to their own ungodly lusts—sensual persons who cause divisions. Jude's forewarning was to believers [Jude 1:16-18].

We are seeing that more and more with the apostate, false church rising up. This false church is embracing the LGBTQ+ movement.

These churches have implemented policies that are inclusive of alternate lifestyles. We now have men who dress up in drag, calling themselves pastors, who are appeasing their sexual brokenness, instead of embracing the Cross to set them free from their bondage. These fallen men and women are void of truth, purity and have no fear of God upon them. Therefore, they have been deceived and believe their unholy lifestyles are actually pleasing to a holy God.

## Highway of Holiness

But for those who choose to walk on the highway of holiness, they can be certain that they will suffer for it. And, equally, our sufferings will produce the patience and endurance that is needed for our character to mature into His likeness. Our sufferings are meant to lead us into holiness by causing our character to mature and be like His [Romans 5:3-4].

**ISAIAH 35:8**
*A highway shall be there, and a road, and it shall be called the Highway of Holiness. The unclean shall not pass over it, but it shall be for others. Whoever walks the road, although a fool, shall not go astray.*

**2 TIMOTHY 3:12**
*Yes, and all who desire to live godly in Christ Jesus will suffer persecution.*

So what does holiness look like in our lives? Holiness suffers long and is kind, it does not envy, it is not puffed up, nor behaves rudely. Holiness does not seek its own way, is not provoked, thinks no evil, does not rejoice in iniquity but rejoices in the truth, bears all things, hopes all things, endures all things. It displays humility. It makes itself of no reputation and will not save its life, but will lose it all for Love's sake. Holiness is the tangible manifestation of His love and grace flowing in our lives and into others' lives, bringing transformation to our spirit, soul and body [1 Corinthians 13:4-7, Philippians 2:7, Matthew 16:25].

But if we cling to Babylon and the unclean places of our souls: pride, rebellion, offenses, jealousy, anger, bitterness, unforgiveness as some examples, we will end up wasting the redemptive purpose for our trials and tears. Equally, our unholiness will cause us to be in unholy alliances. We will end up in relationships that were never His will for our lives. And those relationships will draw us further away from truth and the eternal plans that He has for us. That is not His perfect will or desire for anyone.

Our tests and trials are not only meant to be redemptive, but are meant to prepare us to be the Bride of Messiah; a Bride who will touch the heart of God. The Lord is going to marry a pure and spotless Bride, who has clothed herself in the array of the beauty of His holiness, on this side of eternity. He is not going to marry a harlot bride who has one foot in His Kingdom and the other foot in this world. Our consecration to holiness is vital for the Sanctifier to be able to sanctify us wholly—spirit, soul and body.

## End Result of Faith

I used to think that sanctification and consecration were interchangeable, until the Lord gave me greater understanding many years ago. If we are to be the Bride, then we must live a life of sanctification and 100% consecration. This lifestyle can only come about if we are willing to deny ourselves, take up our cross and follow the Lamb wherever He may lead. For the only way to the glory is through the Cross.

As believers, we need to understand that our salvation is not complete at our new birth. When many people hear the word, "salvation," they think it means a person is saved, and that is all that it means. But being saved is just the first step of a Christian's journey, for without it, we could go no further in His plans. It would be more accurate to say that our salvation has stages that we are expected to walk though, with the goal being that we would receive the end result our faith, the salvation of our souls.

**1 PETER 1:9**
*Receiving the end of your faith — the salvation of
your souls.*

**1 PETER 1:9 AMP.**
*[At the same time] you receive the result (outcome,
consummation) of your faith, the salvation of your souls.*

By this verse, we can see that there is a beginning and an end to
our faith. Therefore, there is a beginning and an end to our salvation.
In Greek, the word for "end" is "telos." It does not mean an end of
something, like it stops. Instead, it means: goal, purpose, fulfillment.
So the end of our faith—or purpose, is the salvation of our soul – or
for our soul to be completely purified. For this is the main reason
why God gave us faith, so that we would come into the fullness of
our salvation, with our souls – or minds renewed, transformed until
Messiah has been completely formed within us.

At our new birth, we have the Seed of Messiah inside of us. We
are a new creation with His DNA inside of us, but that Seed is in its
infantile stage. For it to grow and mature, we have to allow our soul to
be 'saved,' meaning: to be purified from our sin nature. For at our new
birth, our souls were not saved. James tells us to receive the power of
the Word that our soul may be saved.

**JAMES 1:21**
*Therefore lay aside all filthiness and overflow of
wickedness, and receive with meekness the implanted
word, which is able to save your souls.*

James is talking to believers in this verse, not the unsaved. It is
vital that we understand that our salvation was not complete once
when we got saved. It is complete in the sense that it is a finished
work on the Cross, and every provision that we need to come into
the fullness of that finished work has been given to us. But it is not
complete, in that we do not tangibly have the full stature of Messiah

developed into our souls when we are first saved. We are only manifesting a portion of it, not the fullness of it.

> **EPHESIANS 4:13**
> *till we all come to the unity of the faith and of the knowledge of the Son of God, to a perfect man, to the measure of the stature of the fullness of Christ;*

It has always been the Father's plan that we would grow and mature until the full stature of Messiah is within us. He wants us to become mature sons of God, for He desires for us to rule and reign with Him, but it is not automatic. A good father, on this earth, would not let his child drive a car without having the training they needed that would qualify them to know how to drive it. So, too, our Father in heaven is not going to let us rule and reign with Him until we have learned to become like Him, in our words, thoughts and deeds [Job 1:6, Revelation 20:6].

## Three Main Stages to Salvation

This earth is our training ground to learn to reign with Him, by overcoming the obstacles He has left in our path, His way. For it is those who overcome and become mature sons of God, who will receive the full inheritance from the Father. Our getting saved is the first step to becoming a mature son of God. That first step, when we receive Yeshua into our hearts, gets us out of hell. It is a free gift. There is nothing that we can do to earn it. In 2 Thessalonians 2:13-14, we see that there are three main stages to our full salvation:

> **2 THESSALONIANS 2:13-14**
> *But we are bound to give thanks to God always for you, brethren beloved by the Lord, because God from the beginning **chose you for salvation** through **sanctification** by the Spirit and belief in the truth, to which He called you by our gospel, for the **obtaining of the glory** of our Lord Jesus Christ.*

## First Stage: Justification

The first stage is justification. We are justified by faith and the redemptive work of the Cross – His blood atones for our sin. We are saved by believing in our hearts that God raised Yeshua from the dead and by confessing with our mouth that He is Messiah and that His blood atones for our sins. This is the first stage of our salvation, which every new believer in Messiah experiences.

> **ROMANS 3:24, 28, 10:9-10**
> *Being justified freely by His grace through the redemption that is in Christ Jesus, therefore we conclude that a man is justified by faith apart from the deeds of the law. That if you confess with your mouth the Lord Jesus and believe in your heart that God has raised Him from the dead, you will be saved. For with the heart one believes unto righteousness, and with the mouth confession is made unto salvation.*

## Second Stage: Sanctification – Our Purification

The second stage is sanctification. It is the purification stage. It is the process where in which our soul gets saved by the renewal of our mind. Primarily, by how we respond or react to the trials, afflictions and sufferings that we all go through in life. Every believer should be walking through this process. Our trials were not meant to destroy us, but to be redemptive and transform us, if we respond according to the Spirit and not react according to our flesh.

This is the bigger part of a believer's journey. It becomes a lifestyle of choices that we make every day, whether or not to surrender our will for His will, according to the Word – according to His ways, and not man's. Mind and soul, for the most part, can be interchangeable in scripture. And our consecration and sanctification are intimately connected to the renewal of our minds, and that process is intimately connected to how holy we will conduct our lives.

The Lord wants transformation to take place in our daily lives. Without it, we will stagnate. We will not grow and mature into the fullness of His stature. Transformation is vital if we are to know the perfect will of God. If we are not going through stage two, this purification process, we will make decisions based on the unhealed wounds and deceptions of our soul. We will walk after our flesh and not after the Spirit. We will miss the high call that is on our lives to know Messiah, by sharing in the fellowship of His sufferings, so that we would be conformed to His death. In this, we can know the power of His resurrection!

> **PHILIPPIANS 3:10**
> *That I may know Him and the power of His resurrection, and the fellowship of His sufferings, being conformed to His death,*

A resurrection can only take place after a death. If we are not willing to die to our needs, wants and desires – our will, we will not be filled with His glory, which is what transforms us by one degree to the next. The Lord longs to pour His glory into us. But it is not automatic. To the degree that we are willing to be empty of ourselves, will be to the degree which He can fill us with His glory. If He filled us with His glory in our unrefined and impure heart condition, it would kill us. He cannot mix His holiness with our filth. He cannot put new wine in old wineskins.

## Third Stage: Glorification

The third stage is glorification. As we walk through stage two, our soul gets purified. We become more like Yeshua in word, thought and deed. As we behold Yeshua, meditating on the Word, and living a lifestyle of prayer, our mind will be renewed. Our soul will be transformed by one degree of glory after another being filled with His Light. We become more compatible with His divine nature.

**2 Corinthians 3:18**
*But we all, with unveiled face, beholding as in a mirror the glory of the Lord, are being transformed into the same image from glory to glory, just as by the Spirit of the Lord.*

We move further away from the lust of the eyes, the lust of the flesh, and the pride of life, where the spirit of this world no longer holds our souls in captivity. For we move increasingly towards truth, purity, holiness and into a deeper, more intimate walk with the Lord. It does not mean we are there yet, because we are not. But we are now walking on the narrow road that leads to life, where the things of this world no longer attract us, and returning to our former habits are no longer an option. For our previous lifestyle is no longer desirable to us, no matter how hard the narrow road can be to walk upon at times.

**Matthew 7:13-14**
*Enter by the narrow gate; for wide is the gate and broad is the way that leads to destruction, and there are many who go in by it. Because narrow is the gate and difficult is the way which leads to life, and there are few who find it.*

These are the three main stages of salvation that He desires every Christian to go through. If we do, then we will become like Him in character and will come into union with Him. Sadly, most Christians do not get past stage one. They have either no desire to know Him and to go on to glory, or they have been wrongly taught that it is automatic. It is impossible, though, to go on to stage three – glorification – to be the Bride of Messiah, if we are not willing to go through stage two, the sanctification and purification process.

## Salvation is a Process

So, salvation is a process—it is a journey. The Lord could have saved our souls when we became a new creation, which would have made it a lot easier for Him and for us. Instead, in His infinite wisdom, He left our souls in the unsaved – impure state, to draw us out of darkness and into His Light and into a deeper, more intimate, love relationship with Him. In this relationship, we willingly let Him do this deep work in our souls. And to help us to know what needs to be refined in our souls, He allows sufferings to come into our lives, for they expose the tares of our hearts – the sin, wrong thoughts and hurts that need to be uprooted.

But He will not do this uprooting against our will. That is why these 'tares' have been left intact at our new birth. It is not because He is cruel, unkind or forgetful, but the opposite is true. He created us to co-partner with Him and longs to work with us together, to root out those destructive things, which can destroy our souls. He wants to set us free from them by our wills coming into alignment with His in every area of our lives. For He has called us to perfection – to spiritual maturity, which Paul spoke of in Hebrews.

> **HEBREWS 6:1 AMP.**
> *Therefore let us go on and get past the elementary stage in the teachings and doctrine of Christ, advancing steadily toward the completeness and perfection that belong to spiritual maturity...*

## Sanctification and Consecration Work Together

As we walk out the three stages of full salvation: justification, sanctification and glorification, we can see that stage two – our sanctification and purification, is where we will spend a lot of time, working out our salvation with the Lover of our souls. While doing so, sanctification and consecration will work together to bring about His eternal plans, purposes and desires in and through us. So, how do sanctification and consecration differ?

**Sanctification:** is a work that only the Holy Spirit can do within us. When we repent of sin, the Sanctifier of truth comes and cleanses us from that sin. We cannot do that work, only He can. It positions us to keep making choices of consecration, moving us more and more towards truth, holiness and purity.

**Consecration:** is the lifestyle choices that we make to follow and obey truth, to be pure and holy. In its simplest form, it means to be set apart to something. That can be either good or bad. In a believer's life, it is the everyday choices that we make, to be set apart for God's purposes to manifest in our lives. At the same time, many believers have consecrated themselves – set themselves apart, to follow after the spirit of the world, whether they realise it or not. Therefore, consecration is a choice that we make to be separated to something that is either good or bad. And those choices will either cause us to move towards holiness or towards the world's ways of doing things.

**1 PETER 1:15-16**
*He who called you is holy, **you also be holy in all your conduct**, because it is written, "Be holy, for I am holy."*

Both have the meaning to be separated, and the two work together. You cannot have one without the other. Consecration comes when we make a choice to be separated, holy unto the Lord in an area of our lives. It is not always sin that is a stumbling block. Often, it is simply a choice in how we spend our time. Are we willing to let go of distractions, no matter how well-meaning they can appear, but are stopping us from fulfilling His eternal purposes for our lives? Our consecration unto holiness is vital if we are to be filled with the glory. We will decide by our lifestyle choices, for He will not go against our free will.

## A More Consecrated Life

Initially, we may not feel any different when we make choices to live a more consecrated life unto Him. But I can assure you that the Sanctifier is at work, cleansing areas of your soul that have been polluted by the things of this world. He is filling your soul with His Light, causing your mind to be renewed and transformed into His likeness, by one degree of glory to the next. For every time we surrender an area of our lives – by the choices we make, an impartation of the Living God, Who is Light, enters that area of our soul. He comes and sanctifies and purifies it. When that happens, that area of our soul is transformed, and we become more like Him. That is how sanctification and consecration work together. It begins with a choice we make. And behind every righteous choice is the power of God to perform it. Be encouraged, for He gives us the desires to want to be holy, and then He does that work within our soul, as we yield.

> **PHILIPPIANS 2:12-13**
> *Therefore, my beloved, as you have always obeyed, not as in my presence only, but now much more in my absence, work out your own salvation with fear and trembling; for it is God who works in you both to will and to do for His good pleasure.*

## Moving Towards Holiness

We should be constantly moving more towards holiness and further away from sin, wrong thoughts and impure motives. Sanctification and consecration should be operating in our lives every day. We should be moving further away from the lusts and pleasures of this world. When we do, we are moving towards holiness becoming vessels of noble use for the Master.

**2 Timothy 2:20-21 Amp.**

*But in a great house there are not only vessels of gold and silver, but also [utensils] of wood and earthenware, and some for honorable and noble [use] and some for menial and ignoble [use]. So whoever cleanses himself [from what is ignoble and unclean, who separates himself from contact with contaminating and corrupting influences] will be a vessel set apart and useful for honorable and noble purposes, consecrated and profitable to the Master, fit and ready for any good work.*

As a believer, we are the temple of a living and holy God, Who desires to dwell within us. But He can only do so if we are willing to come out of Babylon and leave our unclean and idolatrous ways behind – those things that are not profitable to our soul, nor to His Kingdom. To the degree that we are willing to be purified by His Refiner's fire, is the degree to which He can dwell within our soul. When we are willing, He sanctifies and purifies those areas of our soul. Paul tells us to come out of the unclean places that are harming our relationship with the Lord and with each other, and to cleanse ourselves from everything that is filthy.

**2 Corinthians 6:16-17, 7:1**

*And what agreement has the temple of God with idols? For you are the temple of the living God. As God has said: "I will dwell in them and walk among them. I will be their God, and they shall be My people." Therefore "Come out from among them and **be separate**, says the Lord. Do not touch what is unclean, and I will receive you." Therefore, having these promises, beloved, **let us cleanse ourselves from all filthiness of the flesh and spirit, perfecting holiness** in the fear of God.*

## Come Out of Babylon

The Lord is calling His people out of Babylon. In this late hour, He desires, as never before that we remove the idols of our hearts and to put away all uncleanliness, falsehood, futility and emptiness; thus, holiness can be perfected in our lives. He is calling forth a Bride, who will have no other lovers. And, if we are willing to do so, this bridal preparation will prepare us for these last days that are only getting darker.

In December 2021, the word of the Lord came to me concerning Babylon:

*"The shakings are increasing, as they increase it is more vital than ever before to keep your eyes on Me. The darkness is increasing but My Light is arising—coming forth in those vessels who consider Me worth knowing. Those vessels who have been willing to sit in My Refiner's fire until all the dross has been burned off and out of the deepest recesses of their souls. Few are willing in this hour to be refined. Few walk in integrity of heart before Me. Even fewer walk in the holiness that is required to see My face. As the shakings increase in the days, months and years to come, when My people have seen how they have put their hope, faith and trust in princes of this earth and man-made chariots and how they have failed them – then and only then will they be willing to be cleansed from the Babylonian system that they have loved. Keep calling My people out of Babylon. Keep calling My people to repentance. Keep calling My Bride in this land to come forth without spot or wrinkle. Keep calling My people back to truth, purity, holiness and the fear of God. For without holiness no one will see My face."*

The Lord expects us to be holy, pure, consecrated – set apart, vessels who will be about the Father's business, doing His will on this earth. The traps and snares of this world can cause us to lose our way.

Ungodly thoughts, movies, computer games, gambling, smoking, foul language, anger, unforgiveness, romance novels, pornography and all kinds of sexual sin, lying, gossiping, grumbling and complaining are just a few of the things that trap and ensnare our souls. Every Christian will have to pass through Galatians 5:19-21, with the goal not to have any of the works of the flesh manifesting in our lives.

> **GALATIANS 5:19-21 AMP.**
> *Now the doings (practices) of the flesh are clear (obvious): they are immorality, impurity, indecency, Idolatry, sorcery, enmity, strife, jealousy, anger (ill temper), selfishness, divisions (dissensions), party spirit (factions, sects with peculiar opinions, heresies), Envy, drunkenness, carousing, and the like. I warn you beforehand, just as I did previously, that those who do such things shall not inherit the kingdom of God.*

## God of Peace Will Sanctify Us

As we come out of those unclean places, by crucifying our flesh, we will see an increase of the fruit of the Spirit in our lives. But it requires our response every day. We have to be intentional, if we are to be holy in all of our conduct. When we do, the Holy Spirit and the God of peace will sanctify us wholly. He starts bringing oneness to our spirit, mind and body. There is a 'rest' that we come into, when we understand and yield to this process. It can be painful, lonely and confusing. To those around us, our lives may look like a mess, because they judge us by this world's standards, and not by what the Word teaches and what God expects of us.

> **1 THESSALONIANS 5:23**
> *Now may the God of peace Himself sanctify you completely; and may your whole spirit, soul, and body be preserved blameless at the coming of our Lord Jesus Christ.*

But when we yield, we have a peace that surpasses all understanding, because we will know we are in the perfect will of God. We will know that He wants us to become like Him in word, thought and deed, and that He is able to transform us with the grace that has been given to us to do so.

Yeshua came to set the captives free. He wants us free from those areas in our lives that are holding us captive. It is why this process of sanctification and consecration is vital to our walk, for it causes our conduct on this earth to become holy.

Without going through the sanctification and consecration process, we will not see our faults that need correcting. We will not be willing to be corrected. We will not be able to hear the Lord's voice clearly. In these last days, we cannot afford not to hear His voice clearly. We must put away all compromise and mixture by making choices to be holy, separated unto Him, until the God of peace makes us whole in all areas of our lives. It is vital if we are to touch the heart of God and come before Him with clean hands and a pure heart in that deep place of intercession. It is vital if we are to see the Lord, for without holiness no one will see the Lord. AMEN!

# CHAPTER 6

# CALLED, CHOSEN & FAITHFUL

*These will make war with the Lamb, and the Lamb will overcome them, for He is Lord of lords and King of kings; and those who are with Him are called, chosen, and faithful* [Revelation 17:14].

Faithfulness is a character attribute that is necessary to know the Lord intimately and to be able to touch His heart. It is vital, if we are to be the Bride of Messiah. It is a character trait that takes years to form into a person's soul – into their character, as it can only be proven over time. In His faithfulness to help us become faithful people, He determines the eternal relationships that we are to have on this earth before we are ever formed in our mother's womb. And He uses those relationships to prove our hearts to see if we will remain faithful to them.

There are many types of relationships where our faithfulness is tested: our friendships, our jobs, our church or ministry relationships, our times of devotion and prayer, with parents, siblings and children, our businesses, and especially in our marriages.

**How could we define faithfulness?** Reliable and consistent, unwavering in devotion, consistent with fact or reality; not false, true to one's word, promise or vows regardless of extenuating circumstances.[12]

I do not know anyone who wants to be in a relationship with someone who is not faithful to them or to the purpose of that relationship. For no one likes being betrayed, or thrown under the bus, yet we do it to others all the time, whether we realise it or not.

> **How could we define betrayal?** The breaking or violation of a presumptive contract, trust, or confidence that produces moral and psychological conflict within a relationship amongst individuals or groups. In other words, when someone you trust breaks that trust by doing something that hurts you, often by failing to keep or honor a promise.[13]

Faithfulness is greatly to be desired in our relationships. Yet often it is lacking. When we get tired of something, or things do not turn out as we had hoped, many walk away from the very ones who are meant to help refine their soul to become like Him in this area of faithfulness. When scorching trials come and because roots are shallow, most run from the source of their pain, sorrow, rejection, disillusionments or disappointments. They convince themselves it is the right thing to do. They look for love or comfort in the wrong places by surrounding themselves with those who will tell their broken hearts, bruised egos and itching ears what they want to hear.

It is why we must know the eternal relationships God has for our lives. When we do, we will not abandon them when they go through seasons of pruning. Those relationships are not always known to us from the beginning. Some are easier to identify: parents, children, siblings or marriage partners. And He proves our faithfulness through our earthly relationships to see if we can be found faithful, not only to be the Bride of Messiah, but to steward the gifts, anointings and resources that are needed to complete the works we have been sent to this earth to do.

**Luke 16:10-12**

*He who is faithful in what is least is faithful also in much; and he who is unjust in what is least is unjust also in much. Therefore if you have not been faithful in the unrighteous mammon, who will commit to your trust the true riches? And if you have not been faithful in what is another man's, who will give you what is your own?*

## Our Eternal Relationships

Our eternal relationships will mature over time and produce His character in us, if we do not abort them prematurely. They will also mature if we learn to die to our preconceived ideas of what we ever thought our lives are to look like or feel like, while in those relationships. And especially when those in our lives are not faithful to us or very lovable. It is easier to be faithful to those who treat us well, but it can be quite difficult when the opposite is true. His ways are not ours, nor His thoughts our own but we need them to be, if we are to understand how important faithfulness is to Yeshua and to the Father.

Early in life, at the age of eight, I had received the gift of salvation and was speaking in tongues. In my early teens, I did not have much to do with God, other than believing in Yeshua, and that heaven and hell were real. Because of the unhealthy, dysfunctional family that I grew up in, I dealt with my pain and confusion by pursuing horses during my teen years—it was my escape. I lived and breathed horses, which eventually caused me to come to Ireland in the early 1980's to pursue a British Horse Society Assistant Instructors Certificate.

I met my husband to be during this time and we married about a year and a half later. Neither one of us was walking with the Lord and our lives were full of the world. For the first 13-years our marriage was good, or at least I thought so. About a year before it fell apart, I had started praying to the Lord. I had my own freelance business and things were going really well. I would often thank Him for the business, that I could choose whom I worked for and work half the hours and make twice as much. My prayers were simple prayers of gratitude. Nothing deep and nothing that was causing me to turn my heart back to Him wholeheartedly.

Then everything in our marriage fell apart! The cracks were there all the time, I just could not see them until one day I found out my husband's affections were no longer for me but for another woman. And as I later discovered – other women! The pain of betrayal cut straight through my heart and every muscle, nerve, fiber, ligament and bone in my body. We had made a deal when we married and that deal was, if either one was ever unfaithful, that was it – end of marriage!

## A Painful Time

It was a very painful time, where I just wanted to die. Soon after, I received the Lord into my heart after my sister-in-law offered to pray for me. Although my life was a mess in more ways than one, I now had hope. And I was going to need it, for within days of my husband leaving, my dad called to tell me he had disinherited me. This is how I came back into the Kingdom of God: broken, feeling destroyed and barely holding on, realising I had not really known the love of a father or a husband, and now both had forsaken me.

At one point, my mom, in her hurt for her daughter and wanting to protect me, told me that I needed to divorce my husband. I yelled at her across the room, saying, *"I am not going down the same road of bitterness that you went down with dad. I am choosing forgiveness – to forgive my husband, and if you cannot support me where I am right now, then I do not need you in my life right now."* It was the best I could muster up in my infantile stage as a believer. I was fighting to hold on to whatever God was wanting to do with my life, which at that time, I had no idea!

I just knew, at that time, that if my husband wanted a divorce, I was going to be faithful to our marriage vows until either his or my death. For I had made a covenant with him, until death do we part.

Out of my love for the Lord, I wanted to honour His Word and my covenant, and my doing so was not conditional on whether or not my husband honoured it.

The irony, in my unsaved state, was that I had told my husband that our marriage would be over, under these exact circumstances. But when the Holy Spirit gets a hold of a tender, yielding heart, who no longer wants to live life their own way, He is able to turn that heart all the way around to do the things that please Him.

## The Crucified Life

This was the beginning of learning what it meant to live the crucified life, though I was not familiar with that term; but in fact, I was living out that lifestyle. At the same time, the Lord started speaking to me through dreams, although I had no understanding of the prophetic, either. But He would be faithful to give dreams, forewarning me of situations, and they would play out exactly as I had dreamed. I did not know it then, but He gave me those dreams so I could pray into them.

After a few months of trying to reconcile, my husband chose to live his life separately, but he never pursued a divorce. During that time, the Lord was working on my heart, and particularly where I had failed in our marriage. A couple of times, He had me humble myself before my husband and ask him to forgive me for the pain that I had caused him. The Lord had explicitly instructed me not to make this about my pain, but about the pain I had caused him. Other than those times, we might speak once or twice a year.

Years went by and one evening, while sitting with the Lord, I was contemplating this walk of being faithful to one who is not faithful. Then I asked Him, *"Lord, what good is this walk of faithfulness, if one man's soul cannot be saved, or others around do not see the benefit of it – the restoration of our marriage?"* I further said, *"Lord, if it comes down to his soul being saved or the marriage being restored, save his soul. And if for some reason that does not happen, I like to think I will be okay. That I would not walk away from You, but I do not know."*

When I said that to the Lord, it was not in self-pity, nor did I dwell on it. It was a one-time thought, where even at the time, I had thought it odd, as I do not waver easily. For me, it was the end of the conversation until years later, when my husband got saved after having a powerful open heavens experience, while waiting for a heart transplant in the Mayo Hospital.

The Lord had shown him many things about these last days and given him several words straight from the Father's throne. One time, Peter repeated to me the exact conversation that I had years earlier with the Lord, which no one could have known about, except the Lord. He told me, *"The Lord wants you to know that if I am to die, that I know Him. He wants you to know that you have great faith, and that there is very little faith like yours on the earth and He does not want it to be shaken."* This was how I found out that my husband had been saved. The tears were streaming!

Prior to this moment, the Lord had merged our lives back together after nine years of separation. It came about when my husband had a stroke that had affected his ability to see fully out of one eye, and he reached out for help. It became a season of taking care of him and my dad, who was in a nursing home, while working full-time. During this time, my husband still lived in his apartment entangled in relationships that were of the world and quite destructive. Despite our separate lifestyles, I faithfully prayed for my husband and felt at times like I was a 'lifeline' in his life; praying for him to live and not die. For at that time, he was not saved.

## Constant Rejection

Suffice to say, it was a painful time, where I constantly had to come face-to-face with the rejection that wanted to destroy my soul. Because of our separation, Peter had no idea that I had changed, by living my life for the Lord. In his mind, I was the same person, whom he left nine years earlier. We had a lot of unresolved issues. And when I was misunderstood, I was to do whatever the Lord wanted me to do. Often that meant not making it about my hurt feelings, and keep showing love to one who was not capable to love others, His way, yet. At times, it was humiliating and confusing as our worlds collided, trying to surrender my will for His will.

Peter was not a mean person, or normally unkind. The opposite was true. He did not have a temper and would never want to hurt a flea, and he really had a soft heart. He would go to great lengths to help others. He was one of the nicest and funniest human beings anyone could ever meet. He never put pressure on me to help him and I always knew that if I had chosen to walk away, in his heart of hearts, he would never have blamed me for doing so. He just was not interested in our marriage being restored and lived his life that way. There were times, I would cry all the way home and it was a 22-mile drive, one-way.

When Peter told me that he knew the Lord, about a month before his surgery, I thought, *"Finally, our marriage will be restored and it will only get better going forward."* But I could not have been more wrong. Instead, it was now my time to really die to whatever I ever thought my marriage was going to look like after my husband believed in Yeshua!

During those years of separation, after the Lord had shown me my faults in the marriage, I had asked Him to give me the opportunity to be the wife to my husband that I was always supposed to have been for him. The Lord answered that prayer, by giving me one opportunity after another to die to all of my expectations of my marriage, while creating a peaceful, loving home environment where Peter would feel welcomed, loved and a place where he would want to run to, and not from, no matter what difficulties we might face together.

## Hard to My Flesh

It was extremely hard to my flesh. We walked through very difficult situations, where most would have walked away. But the Lord would not let me. Instead, He would remind me that He never walks away from us, but we are the ones who walk away from Him.

He had put a knowing in my heart that there was a much higher purpose as to why He was allowing me to suffer the emotional pain, sorrow and brokenness, although I did not understand.

Some nights, I cried all night long, thinking that I cannot do this one second longer – the pain is too great. Every time, He would dry my tears and instill deep within my soul that this was all working for my good. And somehow, I just knew beyond knowing that He would never do anything to hurt me, and I believed somehow, this has to be for my good. He would comfort my bruised heart and kept giving me the grace to stay engaged in the relationship, His way.

During this time, the Lord made it clear that it would not be by what I said to my husband, but by my actions towards him. And that how I respond to him will speak louder than any words I could ever speak to him. This meant that often, I would run to the Lord and pour out my sore heart to Him and let Him minister to my needs. He was teaching me to love unconditionally and tangibly, as He loves us, and not as an ideal in one's mind.

When Peter saw that I did not blow up, pout or not talk to him for days, as I had done prior to our separation, he could not recognise this person, who he thought he knew. He could not understand how I could remain in that place of unconditional love, not reacting like I did before towards him. It was all grace, upon grace, with layers and layers of my flesh peeling off, every time! If I had reacted to him, as I did prior to our separation, he would have left, and we both would have missed out on God's eternal plans to be worked into our lives. His ways are truly not our own.

### To Live and Not Die!

After Peter's open heavens experience that he had in late August of 2008, and prior to his transplant two months later, the Lord showed and spoke to him about the day he was to die. That day was August 2, 2008. The Lord took him in the Spirit back to the intensive care unit that he was in that day, and let him overhear the two doctors' conversations. One said, *"I do not think he is going to make it."* The other said, *"I do not think he is going to make it through the night."* He then let him see his soul, how it was barely a flicker of light—it was going out. He let him feel his organs shutting down. The Lord told him, *"Your soul was coming back to me that day. You had rejected Me over and over again. You broke My heart. If it was not for Tracy's prayers, you would not be alive now. She was like a child in a candy shop and would not let go of Me, wanting you to live and not die."*

The Lord had told him how I had suffered great loss earlier in that year, and when I had helped him during those four months, how he had treated me terribly, but that did not stop me from helping him. For which, Peter was truly sorry and repentant. The Lord told him that I had given sacrificially to help him. And because of it, the Lord wanted me to know *"That my reward is very great, for I was the one who got him to that place where he could hear the Lord's voice."* I wept like a baby, telling Peter that I had never done it for a reward, and that this was never on my mind! That day, when I dropped Peter off at his apartment after an appointment with his cardiologist, neither one of us knew if he was going to be alive the next day, for the Lord had answered my prayer and Peter had accepted the Lord as his Savior.

**1 Corinthians 4:1-2**
*Let a man so consider us, as servants of Christ and stewards of the mysteries of God. Moreover it is required in stewards that one be found faithful.*

Thankfully, Peter and I had another two and a half years together. It was a fiery trial like no other! I am eternally grateful to have been given the opportunity to try to be the wife that he deserved to have, and for the opportunity to become His love that one might be saved. Peter's death in 2011 was unexpected; he was healthier than ever and in a good place with the Lord.

There is much more to this story, but I pray that you are starting to see the bigger picture and just how important our faithfulness is to the Lord. For without it, we cannot touch His heart, because we will live a selfish, self-absorbed life, waiting for an apology that may never come. And while doing so, we will miss the greatest opportunity, not to only die to our worthless ways of doing things, but to bring forth resurrection life into those things that only He can raise from the dead in other people's lives!

## Marriage a Divine Tool

Early in my walk, the Lord had given me a dream, where He showed me how our earthly marriage relationship directly correlates to our relationship with Him. Whether saved or unsaved was irrelevant, as His standards do not change in how we are to treat our spouses. He expects all to treat our spouses on this earth, His way. That can be difficult if we do not live a laid-down life unto the Lamb, and it is why so many marriages end in divorce. He showed me that how we treat our spouses reflect how we treat Him. And that marriage was given to mankind to perfect His love into our souls. It was not just for us to have children and pursue the things of this earth. But it is a divine tool to perfect the flaws in our souls that we could come into union with Him. Our earthly marriages are meant to refine our souls, and ultimately, to prepare us to be the Lamb's wife!

> **EPHESIANS 5:31-33**
> *For this reason a man shall leave his father and mother and be joined to his wife, and the two shall become one flesh." This is a great mystery, but I speak concerning Christ and the church. Nevertheless let each one of you in particular so love his own wife as himself, and let the wife see that she respects her husband.*

## A Dire Situation

About four years before the Lord brought my husband back into my life, I became my dad's guardian and conservator. It was a dire situation, where intervention was needed, so that he would not harm himself or others. It meant that his only option was to be moved involuntarily from his home and into a nursing home. It was a hard and emotional time for my family. Because of the years of hurt that my mom and other siblings had towards him, at that time, I was the only one who was able to love him unconditionally. Therefore I became his guardian and conservator.

Despite my own hurt and pain, the Lord had done a wonderful work in my heart after being disowned, and I truly forgave him and stayed in relationship. So in my dad's hour of need, I was the only one who was physically and emotionally able to be involved in his life the way it was needed. I went into this season not expecting anything in return from my dad, but over the next six years, the Lord gave me back my dad – the dad I never had growing up!

This time was a hard transition for him, where often I would be at loss for words, when he would have an understandable melt-down as he tried to come to terms with his loss of freedom. Often all I could say, *"Dad, let's pray to Jesus and see what He will do."* That was all I knew how to do, and so I would pray with him. He was a devout Catholic where prayer was a private matter. So, at first, he was not too happy about praying together, but he eventually warmed up to it.

He deteriorated physically quite quickly. He went in walking, and after a couple of months, he was in a wheelchair where he could do very little for himself. After two years, he was confined to his bed, other than the times they got him up for meals and to shower, or the times I would take him to visit our family or for walks in the park. He was completely dependent upon man to meet his every need, but he was still able to talk clearly and be mentally sound.

Initially, I visited him five or six times a week and then three or four times a week when Peter's health declined. On the weekends, I would hang out, watching old movies with him until he fell asleep. I did his shopping making sure his clothes were in order and bring his favorite comfort foods. I got to know the other residents and the handful of other family members that came faithfully to be with their loved ones. The nursing home became a second home.

Growing up, I loved my dad, but I did not have affectionate feelings for him, for he was absent as a father in every way, other than a physical presence. But one day while taking care of him, I realised that I had these doting affections for him, like a parent would for a child. I adored him and our times together! But my heart hurt, knowing that he had no quality of life. I did not want him to suffer one second longer than necessary. He was not in physical pain, but was unable to do anything.

## Eternal Purpose

Often, I would ask the Lord not to let him suffer one second longer than necessary. I knew everything God did had eternal purpose, so there had to be purpose. One purpose was that my dad's soul would be saved by his flesh being handed over to destruction. And the day came that he got saved—three years later! But he still laid in that bed for another three years and it broke me. On the outside, I could not see the eternal purpose, but knew there had to be one.

I had been pursuing the deeper things of God at this time. I had heard a message on compassion and how, as a believer, we must pursue it and ask for it. I started praying daily for the Lord to give me compassion, knowing I needed it. I prayed that prayer for a few years. Towards the end of dad's life, he was put on Hospice care. During one of my visits, I asked to speak with the hospice nurse, and while I waited, I went to find dad, who was in the dining room eating lunch. I came up from behind, and put my arm around his shoulders and told him that I love him, as I always had. I started to greet his caretaker, who was sitting opposite me. But when I did, I no longer saw her, for the Lord was standing in front of me, dressed in a white robe.

## Compassion

He spoke one sentence to me and was gone.  He said, *"The reason I allowed your dad to suffer this long was to teach you compassion."*

My eyes became rivers overflowing. I looked around at all these precious ones that had no one to visit them. I prayed for their souls. I had before, but it was impressed upon me to do so again. At the same time, it was like a movie screen before my eyes. I saw the times over the past six years, where I had stopped to reach the lonely, the destitute and forgotten ones in that nursing home: to say hello, to hold their hand, to go 'racoon hunting' or to let them embrace my dog's contagious love for them. Often, I was the last one to be with them before they died. I would pray for them, not knowing they would not be there the next day.

My heart was breaking to a billion pieces. The staff thought I was crying because my dad was dying. I was undone and could not wait to leave, as I had to be with the Lord. The thought that my dad had to lay in that bed and suffer for one second, in order for me to learn compassion was unbearable to my emotions. He will always answer prayers that align with His will, in ways that are truly not our ways.

When the Lord spoke that word, it was not a rebuke, for He quickly replayed in my mind's eye what it meant to have compassion. But it was a "letting me know" that this was what it was going to take. Up until that point in my life, I was not comfortable around older people. I did not know how to engage with them. Dad died a little over three months later, two and half months after my husband. I spent the last 13 days of his life sleeping on the floor next to his bed at night, as I did not want him to die alone. I knew the angels and the Lord would be with him, but I wanted to be there when he finished his race and crossed over.

I believe it is immensely important to the Lord that we honour our parents on this earth. He says that if we do, we will have a long life. I know there are situations where it seems impossible for a son or daughter to honour their parents, while they are still alive. But if you have that blessed opportunity to do so, despite how painful the past has been, you will be astounded at what God will do to take what was meant to destroy you and work it for your good!

**HEBREWS 3:5-6**
*And Moses indeed was faithful in all His house as a
servant, for a testimony of those things which would
be spoken afterward, but Christ as a Son over His own
house, whose house we are if we hold fast the confidence
and the rejoicing of the hope firm to the end*

Over the years, my mom and brothers were able to come to a
place of peace with dad, and my dad did eventually re-inherit me,
long after I had let go of that expectation and the hurt that I had
because of it. I am eternally grateful for those six years with dad,
and have no regrets. If I had run and not followed the Lamb, I would
have missed one of the greatest eternal lessons of my life and what
He wanted to teach me—compassion.

Compassion compels us to help set captives free. It causes
our needs to fade into the background, while the needs of others
become our focus. Compassion fuels our prayers and without it, it is
impossible to touch the heart of God. Often, we can learn compassion
in our seasons of being faithful to those who are incapable of loving
us for whatever the reasons.

There are some who are reading this who can relate to what
I have shared. Our situations may not be the same, but the thread
that is woven is the same strand. It is the thread of faithfulness
woven into your soul. Be encouraged and know there is a blessing
that the Lord bestows upon those who remain faithful to the eternal
relationships He has given you, no matter what the cost, and from
a surrendered heart. And, especially, when you think no one else
sees, He sees it all!

For those of you who are parents, I believe the Lord wants to
especially encourage you. Those who have been faithful to raise their
children, knowing Yeshua, but in their adult life they seem to be going
the wrong way. Be encouraged, your efforts have not been in vain.
Your prayers and your tears have been heard and collected. They
will bear good fruit at their appointed time. For He will be faithful to
restore them back to the way, the truth and the life.

## Unoffended Love

Our faithfulness does not mean that we will not get hurt, become angry or rejected at times. It can look like everything in our life is being destroyed. But we do not give up on others, especially when they have given up on us. When we walk in unoffended love and not out of bitterness, unforgiveness or false humility, the Lord can only bless the works of our hands and give us beauty for ashes, all the while qualifying us to be the Bride of Messiah.

We see that with David and the men who were with him when the Amalekites invaded and burned Ziklag with fire. The Amalekites had taken their wives, sons and daughters into captivity. It looked like everything was lost and destroyed. David's men turned against him and were going to stone him. But David did not give up on them. When everything was falling apart all around him, he did not focus on their reactions. He did not have a pity party. Instead, He knew that God was faithful to those who are faithful to Him, and strengthened himself in the Lord. When He did, the Lord was faithful to recover all that seemed lost [1 Samuel 30:1-8].

**1 SAMUEL 30:6**
*Now David was greatly distressed, for the people spoke of stoning him, because the soul of all the people was grieved, every man for his sons and his daughters. But David strengthened himself in the Lord his God.*

What does it mean to strengthen ourselves in the Lord? To remind ourselves of God's Word and promises to us. Both His written Word and the rhema words, which are words spoken into our lives that are to guide us and impart life. It means we do not let go of His promises. Instead, we remain patient in battle, waiting for strategies from heaven to come forth to move us forward.

Faithfulness does not mean that we are perfect in all of our ways, but that we remain faithful to the call. David was faithful to his call to lead Israel in the ways of the Lord, despite committing adultery and murder. He was faithful to repent and bring the Lord the burnt offerings that were due to Him. That speaks of laying aside our fleshly ways of doing things on the altar of sacrifice, so His ways can become our ways. It is costly. It will cost you everything in your life that exalts itself against the knowledge of God.

> **PROVERBS 17:17**
> *A friend loves at all times, and a brother is born for adversity.*

Faithfulness means that we keep showing up. We keep doing what the Lord has asked of us, especially when there is nothing in our weak flesh that wants to do so. We honour our word to those who are not honourable. We love a friend at all times, whether we are in favor or out of favor with them. It means we are reliable, consistent, trustworthy, such that others will know that if we say we are going to do something, we will do it.

> **PROVERBS 12:22 AMP.**
> *Lying lips are extremely disgusting and hateful to the Lord, but they who deal faithfully are His delight.*

> **PROVERBS 20:6**
> *Most men will proclaim each his own goodness, but who can find a faithful man?*

## Gift of Faith

If we remain faithful, our faithfulness to His purposes will cause the gift of faith to operate in our lives. Abraham, Moses, Joshua, Peter and James operated in the gift of faith, displaying His miracle working power in and through them, affecting those around them and those who would come after them. When the gift of faith comes upon you, it will cause you to hold on to the promises of God no matter what your eyes see or flesh feels, for you have absolutely no doubt that what the Lord has spoken will come to pass. There is absolutely nothing that can make you waver.

The gift of faith is necessary, along with all the gifts of the Spirit, in order to manifest His plans on earth, as they exist in heaven. I firmly believe that one way He qualifies His Bride is by giving her a promise – a personal word for his or her life, church or ministry, where it will look like it will never come to pass. In the natural, there is nothing possible to make it happen, but they hold on to that promise until it manifests. He loves to do the impossible with those who believe like Mary and say, *"Let it be done unto me, according to Your word."* When we do, the gift of faith will cause His supernatural power to manifest those plans into our lives.

## The Proving of Our Hearts

Faithfulness is one of the fruits of the Spirit. Therefore, He will prove His Bride's heart to see if she will remain faithful. And especially when betrayed, rejected and forsaken by the very ones who should love her the most. A servant is not greater than his or her Master. And if He was rejected, betrayed, mocked, scorned and forsaken by man, we can be certain that His Bride – those called and chosen, will go through similar situations. He allows it to sift through the layers of our hearts, to purge out our unfaithfulness. For He is going to marry a Bride who is faithful to Him.

Traveling the narrow road and striving to enter through the narrow gate is not easy. It can be easy to fall into discouragement or disillusionment when contending to complete the works our Father has for us to do. But self-pity – our pity parties, will do nothing to promote God's plans in our lives. Instead, if we walk in it, it will only promote Satan's plans against our lives. It will stop us from moving forward in God's plans and hurt those around us. We must learn how to encourage ourselves in the Lord, like David. It is a key to becoming and remaining faithful to the Lord, to the Word and to the call that is upon our lives to be molded and formed into His likeness.

We must have the Word of God buried deep within our souls,

so when facing opposition, hardships, disappointments and delays, we will hold onto what is truth and not believe the lies the enemy whispers in our ears. May we never forget that He Who is in us, is far greater than the hordes of hell that are against us. And how the Lord opened Elisha's spiritual eyes and he saw the countless host of heaven's army fighting for him. So too, is it for us, when we remain faithful to the only One called Faithful and True [1 John 4:4, 2 Kings 6:16].

**PROVERBS 25:19**
*Confidence in an unfaithful man in time of trouble is
like a bad tooth and a foot out of joint.*

In difficult times, the Lord proves our hearts to see if we will remain faithful, or if we will take offense with Him, or with others, when everything is falling apart. He will also prove our hearts in the simple things that He asks of us. For example, will we pray every day for the amount of time He sets? Or, maybe it is to meet with Him every day at the same time in the early morning hours—are we willing, will we be found faithful to show up every day?

In 2009, I was in a prayer meeting in Jerusalem where a mighty woman of God was leading the intercessory prayer on a national level. I loved Israel, but at that time I did not know how to pray for Israel and would run out of prayers after ten minutes. This dear sister provoked me like no other. Her prayers were powerful, anointed, tender and beating to the heart of the Father. When I returned home, I told the Lord how I wanted to be able to pray with that same kind of heart burning for Israel. It was not out of envy or competition, but her prayers lit a fire in my heart and I did not want that fire to go out.

The Lord answered by instructing me that I was to pray for Israel for half an hour a day, for one-year. Initially, it was a struggle, for it felt like time moved so slowly. Some days, I just prayed in the Spirit. But within a short time, my prayer time increased, where I no longer felt like time moved slowly. As I persisted, the Lord would give me His burden causing my prayers to flow freely, where I lost sight of time. It would not have happened, if I had not been faithful – consistent and reliable, to show up, despite my lack. Our faithfulness is not passive, but active. It requires our response, and often comes with a price to be paid by those who are willing.

So the Lord will prove our hearts because He wants to know if we will walk away from our first love. Will we look to other lovers to meet our needs, and especially when we are in the wilderness? He wants to know if we will we be faithful when we think no one else sees what we are doing? Will we be faithful to His Word? Will we be faithful to overcome by the blood of the Lamb, by the word of our testimony, and not love our lives, unto death?

**LUKE 12:42-44**
*And the Lord said, "Who then is that faithful and wise steward, whom his master will make ruler over his household, to give them their portion of food in due season? Blessed is that servant whom his master will find so doing when he comes. Truly, I say to you that he will make him ruler over all that he has.*

He wants to know, because He wants to qualify us to reign with Him during the Millennium Reign. For those who are found faithful, He will provide above and beyond what we need to be a vessel of mercy, who brings resurrection life to those who are left for dead. He wants to bring restoration to our relationships and the plans He has for our lives. If we are to touch the heart of God with our intercessions, we must be found faithful to keep asking, keep seeking and keep knocking until His Kingdom comes and His will is done on earth, as it is in heaven.

On Passover 2023, the Lord spoke a word to me concerning faithfulness:

*"I AM faithful to honour My Word to mankind, but faithful to those who are faithful to Me. I say assuredly this day, their eyes will see, their ears will hear and their hearts will understand*

*how great and marvelous are My plans for them and what I will do in and through them."*

May we remain faithful to the eternal plans He has for our lives, so that we can be filled with His glory and clothed in His Light to be a testimony of His faithfulness in these last days. AMEN!

# CHAPTER 7

# OUR PRAYERS, TEARS & INTERCESSIONS

*So I sought for a man among them who would make a wall, and stand in the gap before Me on behalf of the land, that I should not destroy it; but I found no one [Ezekiel 22:30].*

Prayer is the lifeline to the heart of God. It has the ability to affect life and death. Intercessory prayer is a life-saving ministry, for it holds authority and power of life over the enemy's power of death and destruction. Our prayers, tears and intercessions are powerful ways to sow seeds into the Kingdom of God. And, at the same time, that prayer protects, waters and nurtures those seeds, causing them to birth the plans of God at their divinely appointed time for our personal lives, families, cities and nations.

But not all prayer is holy, pure, selfless and acceptable to God. We see an example of this when Yeshua rebuked the Pharisees for devouring widows' houses, covering up their greed with long prayers. Their motive for praying was impure, profane and not pleasing to God. It was for selfish gain at the cost of others' lives being harmed. We saw the prayers of Nadab and Abihu were unholy, costing them their lives before a holy God [Matthew 23:14, Leviticus 10].

## Heaven has Protocols

Heaven has protocols. If our prayers are to be heard and answered, we must follow those protocols to co-partner with a holy and pure God. Many are familiar with 2 Chronicles 7:14. It is an often quoted verse, by those who engage in prayer. But often, I hear it partially quoted. Many leave out the call to turn from our wicked ways. If the Remnant would apply this verse to every area of our lives, the Lord would have come back a long time ago, for His Bride would have made herself ready by getting rid of every spot, wrinkle, blemish or any such things.

> **2 CHRONICLES 7:14**
> *If My people who are called by My name will humble themselves, and pray and seek My face, and turn from their wicked ways, then I will hear from heaven, and will forgive their sin and heal their land.*

If we are to come before a holy God, we must come low and truly broken over the sin in our lives, in our families' lives, in our cities and nations. We must seek His face from a heart posture of humility, acknowledging our wicked ways, by asking for forgiveness of sin, whether in our own lives or by identificational repentance. This type of repentance occurs when we stand in the gap and take on that sin as if it is our own for an individual, situations, communities or our nations. When we do, then we will hear from heaven, then He will forgive our sins and only then can our souls and nations be healed.

> **PSALM 100:4**
> *Enter into His gates with thanksgiving, and into His courts with praise. Be thankful to Him, and bless His name.*

If our prayers are to be heard and answered, we must come boldly into His throne of grace with thanksgiving and praise. It is vital that we learn this protocol. Too many believers start their times of prayer and bypass this glorious step. It is the presence of the Living God that changes lives and circumstances. Prayer is a conduit for that change to take place. There is nothing that will cultivate the presence of God in our times of prayer, whether personal or corporate, more quickly than when we spend adequate time not just in worship, but with prayers that express our gratitude, praise, love and adoration to the King of kings and Lord of lords. As a ministry, in our prayer watches, we can spend a half hour acknowledging His majesty, His glory and just thanking Him before we ever utter one prayer for why we have come before Him.

To help better illustrate, as a parent, when your teenager or adult child comes and ask you to do something for them but they do not thank you, how do you feel? But if they are respectful of your authority and position, knowing that you do not have to do what you do for them, but instead are grateful for the times you have helped them, how is your heart going to feel towards them? If what they are asking is not harmful to them or others but for their good, you will do it joyfully! It is the same with our relationship with Yeshua and with the Father.

**Isaiah 66:2**
*For all those things My hand has made, and all those things exist, says the Lord. But on this one will I look: On him who is poor and of a contrite spirit, and who trembles at My word*

If our prayers are to be heard and answered, we must be a people who walk in the fear of the Lord. For when we do, we will not walk in evil. Instead, we will tremble at His holy Word. Our prayers will be a fountain of life, turning many away from the snares of death. We will guard our hearts, for it is the source of life. We will want to put away all gossip and slander.

Too often, people bring the spirit of the world—pride, anger, bitterness, envy, sexual sin, as examples, into their prayer times. They have not crucified their flesh, by taking every thought captive, therefore, their thought life is polluted and defiled by the spirit of the world that stops them from engaging in their times of prayer from holy ground.

We often invite a holy God to mingle with our filth or worldly ways. Because many do not regard Him as Holy and One to be reverentially feared, our times of prayer are from the flesh and not led by the Spirit of the Living God. But when we walk in the fear of the Lord, it brings the purity that is needed, for purity triggers God's power to move in a reformative and transforming way, whether on a personal or national level [Proverbs 16:6, 14:27, 4:23].

## One Man – One Bride

Ezekiel 22:30 states that if the Lord could find just one man, He would not bring destruction to the land. Have you ever wondered why the Lord said, *"If He could just find one man?"* It was not because there were not people who were willing to pray, because there were many in those days. The issue was about character. He wanted to know if He could find just one man who knew that the Lord cares far greater about our obedience and holiness than any sacrifice that we could bring to Him, when He did not ask for it. For most in those days were not willing to yield their will for His and be refined by His refiner's fire in their words, thoughts and deeds in order to become like Him so that He could save them from destruction.

We see an example of this with the Israelites with their fear, disobedience and murmuring to God's ways, after He had brought them out of Egypt. Joshua and Caleb were the only two that entered the Promised Land, while all the others never entered into the fullness of God's plans for their lives. As it was then, so it still is today, and our characters must become like His, if we are to be used mightily by Him in these last days.

But Abraham, Moses, Joseph, Job, Nehemiah, Daniel, Esther, David and Paul, they all had it—character. They had character that matched His, in order to accomplish His eternal, redemptive purposes on this earth for mankind. All were great, humble leaders, who laid down their lives for the bigger picture, for people and nations to be saved. It was not about saving themselves or their reputations. They were all friends of God, who were allowed to touch His heart. And because of it, they walked in their priestly roles, and not just their kingly roles, and were used mightily as powerful intercessors to bring about God's purposes for their people and nation.

Too often, pastors delegate prayer, if there is prayer at all in their churches, thinking they do not need to be a part of it. We do not see this with Abraham, Moses, Joseph, Job, Nehemiah, Daniel, Esther, David and Paul. They all held positions of prestige and power. They did not delegate the prayer—they were the prayer! And because of it, their people and nation were saved.

Were they any different than any one of us today? "No!" They were laid-down, 100% surrendered vessels who followed the Lamb, wherever He led them. It is an invitation to many, but few are willing; therefore, few are chosen to lead on this level. It was not about them, but about God getting what He deserves. It was about comforting His heart that the nations may be saved.

That is the big picture. God is after a Bride for His Son, who will build up the wall and stand in the gap that our nations would not be destroyed. For the Son will see the fruit of the travail of His soul and be satisfied. He will inherit the nations, and reign with His Bride, who will match Him in character. Prayer was never about numbers, but about the heart – about how pure it is, and what are our motives for praying. God can save a nation with one person. Equally, He will have one Bride – not many, with whom He will co-partner with in these last days to bring about His eternal purposes in the nations.

## Different Types of Prayer

There are many types of prayer. Therefore, not all prayer is the same. Paul states in Ephesians 6:18 that we are to pray always with all prayer and supplication in the Spirit. If he had not said, *"...with **all** prayer..."* we could possibly conclude that there is only one kind of prayer. But prayer is not that simple. On the one hand, it can be simple.

And, on the other hand, it can be complex where it has the ability to uproot strongholds and tear down walls of hardness, to reach the deepest and darkest part of a person's soul or the soul of a nation.

**1 TIMOTHY 2:1**
*Therefore I exhort first of all that supplications, prayers, intercessions, and giving of thanks be made for all men,*

From this verse, we see that there are supplications, prayers and intercessions and prayer is not singular, but plural.

**How could we define prayer?** A broad definition would be: to plead on behalf of another.

**How could we define supplication, or petitions?** Any prayer that asks God for something.[14] Example; *"Lord, please help Mrs. Faith be able to pay her bills."*

**How could we define prayers?** Talking to God. It is our way of communicating our thoughts, needs, and desires to Him. It is an avenue that God has provided for the believer, of making known the deepest feelings of our heart.[15]

**How could we define intercession?** God's brilliant strategy for including the saints in ruling with Him in power. Yet, it has such great impact on us, as it draws us into intimacy with God, protects with humility, transforms with holiness, anoints with power, unifies in community, releases revelation, and increases our inheritance, while it trains us to rule with His wisdom.[16]

Intercessory prayer is to take hold of God and not let go, pleading on behalf of another. The strategies and outcome are often long-term, with many shorter-term breakthroughs along the way. These bring us steps closer to the final victory – or outcome. Yet, there are also times when we have shorter intercessory prayer assignments. For example, when we are interceding for someone who was in an accident and needs life-saving surgery. So intercessory prayer is not always long-term, but can be shorter term, in certain situations.

As an intercessor, we aim to know the will of God for a situation. For when we do, we will keep praying until the breakthrough comes, or we die – whichever comes first! That is the true heart of an intercessor. They know the will of God and refuse to settle for less. They are often what I describe as someone like a pit bull with a bone in its mouth – refusing to let go of it! We see that with Abraham interceding on behalf of Lot.

While one person may pray a two or three-minute prayer for the needs of another, an intercessor will be able to pray that same prayer request for an hour or much more. Both types of prayer are good and acceptable to God and both are needed. But when we are called to that place of intercession and we do not obey, we will have to give an account to God for why we did not obey. Therefore, a two or three-minute prayer may not be how we are to pray, at times. We must become and stay sensitive to the promptings of the Holy Spirit calling us deep unto deep.

## Heartbeat is Compassion

The heartbeat of intercession is compassion. It will bring us to our knees, every time, to cry our heart out for those we know and those we do not know. It can be easy to cry for those we know, but not so easy for someone we do not know, or situations that we have very little understanding of, in the natural. But when our spirit is in tune with the Living God, we will feel what He feels about a person or a situation.

There was a time, while we were separated, when the Lord allowed me to feel my husband's heart by allowing me to know why he chose some of the things that he did while growing up. I felt what he felt, while he walked through those painful moments in his life.

I took on my husband's person, so to speak, and I wept for several days, interceding for him to live and not die. For I understood things about his childhood that no one would have known except him and God, which had negatively affected him his whole life, and were causing him to stumble in his adult life.

> **How could we define Compassion?** A feeling of distress and pity for the suffering or misfortune of another, often including the desire to alleviate it, a disposition to be kind and forgiving.

At the same time, our intercessions require us to be fervent, for it is the effective fervent prayers of the righteous that avails much, not the 'polite' prayers that care what man thinks about them [James 5:16].

> **How could we define fervency?** It is characterised by intense emotion, ardent love, an impassioned appeal, intensely passionate, burning or glowing.

We see an example of this with Moses, who walked in the office of a prophet. He was a prophet and a powerful intercessor, who was broken for his stiff-necked people. A prophet is appointed by the Lord Himself. Today, the prophetic stream is polluted with a lot of self-proclaimed prophets or prophetesses saying, *"Thus says the Lord,"* when the Lord never spoke it. The character of a prophet takes years for the Lord to develop. I shared more about those attributes in *Bewitched & Beguiled: Wolves in Sheep's Clothing*.[17] A true prophet will have the heart of the Father. They will weep and intercede for the very words that the Lord has given them to steward. They are broken vessels who have yielded 100% to the Spirit of God in every area of their lives.

When they speak a hard word, they take no pleasure in doing so. Instead, their hearts are broken to pieces. They are not looking to build their name, their ministry or their reputation. They have one objective: to hear the voice of the Lord and to only speak what He tells them. It is not about them, but all about the Lord getting what He wants from peoples, tribes, tongues and nations. We see this in the lives of Moses, Isaiah, Jeremiah, King David and Paul.

When Israel made the golden calf, and Moses interceded on their behalf, God told him that He was going to destroy all of Israel and would instead make him a great nation. But Moses stood in the gap and pleaded the heart of God to save his people, for he knew the heart of God was not to destroy. Moses reminded the Lord of His promises to Israel and why He should turn His wrath away. He ends this intense time of intercession by saying, if the Lord would not forgive them, for Him to blot his name out of the book of life [Exodus 32].

How many of us today would pray that way? How many pastors or leaders, who have rebellious sheep who have made their lives bitter and difficult, would be willing to have their names blotted out of the book of life for them? Or, for our government leaders who are destroying our nations by following Satan's counsel. I believe most would say, *"Yes, Lord, blot them out, get rid of them. They have been nothing but trouble, refusing to obey You. Make me great instead!"*

The heart of God is to save and not destroy. Moses knew it, and that caused him to boldly, but humbly come before His throne of grace to obtain the mercy they needed. This is why the Lord looks for just one man who will stand in the gap, one who has His heart—His character, towards mankind to save and not destroy. He could have asked for a thousand, a hundred, even ten to do so, but He asks for just one! It is because He does not want to destroy us, but restore us back to the eternal plans and purposes for our lives through that place of intercessory prayer.

**LUKE 9:56, 19:10**
*For the Son of Man did not come to destroy men's lives but to save them. For the Son of Man has come to seek and to save that which was lost.*

We see that it was compassion that propelled the Lord to put aside His glorious identity and lower Himself a little lower than the angels, to walk amongst our filth and brokenness, wanting to save us. He came to seek and restore what has been lost. Compassion drove Him to the Cross. And when dying that horrific death, while the thief and the robber mocked Him, He prayed, *"Father, forgive them, for they know not what they do."* That is the heart of the Father. It is because of the Lord's mercies that we are not consumed because His compassions fail not [Lamentations 3:22].

Moses knew that the Lord's compassions would not let them be destroyed. It is why compassion is vital when we pray. It will cause us to go humbly before His throne of grace fervently, often weeping for others, and for the vilest evil situations to be turned for good. Seeking for Him to bring life, where Satan wants to bring death.

## The Weeping Room

In January 2004, Jennifer Miller Toledo had a vision where the Lord revealed to her the intimacy room, the weeping room and the strategy room. The weeping room was a place where He told her that very few chose to enter because it was not extravagant, it was lonely, it was not comfortable, and a person had to be very low to fit through the door. She had to get on her knees to enter it. Once there, she understood why it was called the weeping room. For on one of the walls there was a small window and the Lord would sit in a chair in front of it, looking out. As He looked out, He heard every human cry coming forth from the earth. He saw all the injustices, the rapes taking place. He heard the cries of the rejected. He heard every prayer and every cry all at the same time. Jennifer was overwhelmed and began to weep. She wept for hours for what was breaking the Lord's heart. As she did, her selfish ambitions faded away.

When she noticed another door that was in the weeping room, she asked the Lord if she could enter it. It was the strategy room. He told her that she would not fit through the door. That she had to first spend time in the weeping room. For it was in the weeping room where her soulish desires would be stripped away until she was small enough to enter. She understood the Divine order, where our intimacy with Him will cause us to surrender ourselves to the weeping room. And when our hearts are proven to break for what breaks His, the King will invite us into the strategy room to receive heaven's counsel to execute His plans on earth, as they exist in heaven. [18]

## Open Invitation

Heaven has protocols and it is not automatic for someone to touch the heart of God, but it is an open invitation to all who are willing to pay the price. Intimacy with Yeshua and the Father are vital if we are to know His heart and be able to touch it. Without it, we will end up building our own kingdoms and not His. As an intercessor we are called to be a "soldier in spirit." Many times, we are called to pray for what is outside realms of our natural possibilities. In order to do so, we must have an intimate relationship with both, Yeshua and the Father.

> **How could we define intimacy?** It generally refers to the feeling of being in a close personal association and belonging together. It is a familiar and very close affective connection with another as a result of a bond that is formed through knowledge and experience of the other. Genuine intimacy requires dialogue, transparency, vulnerability and reciprocity.

The Father and Yeshua want intimacy with us. We were created to be in a love relationship with Him. We cannot relate to the things He shows us without that intimacy. When we first begin to move into that place of intimacy with the Lord, it can be like a culture shock. Some run from it, for it frightens them. For in their childhood, they did not experience healthy, intimate relationships with their parents, other adults or siblings. Today, most in the Church have an unhealthy concept of intimacy; therefore they are far from God's purposes for their lives.

God not only wants intimacy with us, but it is required if we are to touch His heart and be His Bride. Our obedience, humility, purity, holiness, and intimacy are all required to be able to carry His burdens and for us to be vessels of intercessory prayer. Without intimacy, it is not possible to carry His burdens. And that intimacy brings us the protection that we need against Satan when engaging in the battle, because we will know what the will of the Father is for our lives or a situation and not step outside those boundaries.

**PSALM 140:7**
*O God the Lord, the strength of my salvation, You have covered my head in the day of battle.*

At the same time, there are times we will suffer greatly for our intercessions. But He does not send us into the battle without going with us. If we want to be close to the heart of God, we will always face a level of discomfort, but in the discomfort is the heart of God. Intercession is the greatest call on the face of the earth, with Yeshua being our example, for He is forever making intercession before the Father desiring that not a soul would perish. Intercession is a divine love trap. It brings us into Him where we do not want out. It is a mystery—nothing like it!

But one has to be selfless and willing to put aside self. Most often it is our pride and sleep! We have to say goodbye to our own agendas and timings. It can often be inconvenient to let His ways become our ways and His thoughts our own. But when we do, we will experience things in God where others will not because they are not willing to lose their life for the sake of others. It is hard, discouraging at times, with many disappointments along the way. But when you get a glimpse of the Glory, anything this world has to offer pales in comparison! Our intercessions give us the privilege to walk in a Bridal relationship with Yeshua, and before others. It is a place that is so pure, so holy. It is a place full of authority that lives above all evil. It is all grace, upon grace.

## Our Tears

To fully move the heart of God to not let Satan's destruction come upon our lives, families, communities, cities and nations, will take our tears and fastings. Why our tears? Because it is what He requires. We are to come before Him with fasting, weeping and mourning. We are to rend our hearts. As priests, we are to weep between the porch and the altar until the broken fellowship has been restored that He may relent and spare us. The broken fellowship depicts the sin that has caused a breach to come between us and God [Joel 2:12-17].

Our tears demonstrate to Him godly sorrow over our sin, when we confess it before Him. Tears represent a broken, contrite and repentive heart, that wants to turn from their wicked ways. This applies individually, or as we stand in the gap for others, or our cities and nations.

There are only two ways for God to deal with our sin. Either by our repentance and the blood of the Lamb making atonement for us. Or, by judgment coming upon our lives: individually, in our families, communities, cities or nations, because He will bring justice to every situation on earth that is not in alignment with His government. His justice comes to make every wrong right, as only He can do. And before He brings judgment, He gives every people, tribe, tongue and nation ample opportunity to repent that we can avoid the discipline, or wrath of God.

**EZRA 10:1**
*Now while Ezra was praying, and while he was confessing, weeping, and bowing down before the house of God, a very large assembly of men, women, and children gathered to him from Israel; for the people wept very bitterly.*

It is why our intercessory prayer with tears and fasting is a life-giving ministry. For the Lord desires our sin to be covered by the blood of the Lamb—the Cross. And why identificational repentance, as we see in Daniel chapter nine where he confessed his sins and the sins of his people, is needed to move the heart of God to restore and not destroy lives. Identificational repentance is needed, for it will cause mercy to triumph as much as possible over His judgments. It is needed, as those who we are interceding for are lost, blind and left for dead. They have no idea how much they need a Savior and Redeemer, whose name is Yeshua to save them!

It is not His desire to destroy them, but His justice will demand that He makes the wrong things right. He is a holy God who will not always strive with man. This is why our identificational repentance prayers on behalf of the lost are vital, so that His heart can be appeased. And He can move to save, and not destroy them. But when God's judgments come, they are always just, true and righteous. They are always out of His highest redemptive love for mankind, with one motive: to restore us back to truth, to righteousness, to a right relationship with Him and with the Father, not desiring a single soul to perish.

Our tears of repentance can comfort God's heart. They cannot always stop the judgments, but can diminish the death, destruction and desolation that our sin and rebellion bring into our lives and nations. Our tears have a voice in heaven and they are powerful to move the heart of God. We see this in the book of Esther, when Haman had gotten King Ahasuerus to make a law that would annihilate Queen Esther's people—every Jewish man, woman, boy and girl in the king's kingdom. Esther had a strategy from the beginning. Too often our prayers are selfish or a "knee jerk" reaction, based on our emotions and not God's ways of doing things. We need to seek heaven for strategy. It takes strategy to save a nation. Esther depicts this for us.

## Seeking the King

Initially, Esther was in a state of complacency, when she first received the tragic news. For she believed there was nothing she could do when Mordecai told her to seek the king to plead for their people.

For according to the law, anyone who went into the king's inner court without being summoned would be put to death. But Mordecai jolted her out of her complacency by telling her not to flatter herself and think that just because she dwells in the king's palace, that she would escape this death sentence. Further saying, if she remained silent, help would come for the Jews some other way, but you and your father's house will perish. For who knows whether you have come into the kingdom for such a time as this [Esther 4:1-13].

Esther did not flip out emotionally, like most of us would do with such devastating news. Instead, she called for everyone to fast for three days. She was waiting on God for His counsel. She then came before the king on three separate occasions. The first time, she requested to have a banquet with the king and Haman, her enemy. She never spoke a word about the evil plot. The king says that whatever she wants, up to half the kingdom is hers. She requests dinner with them a second time, where she exposes the evil plot against her people. The king agrees, has Haman killed, but there is still a problem. There is a law in place to destroy all of her people and only the king can overturn it [Ester 5:4, 7:1-9].

**ESTHER 8:3**
*Now Esther spoke again to the king, fell down at his feet, and implored him with tears to counteract the evil of Haman the Agagite, and the scheme which he had devised against the Jews*

This is when we see Esther come before the king one more time, falling at his feet, pleading with tears to save her people. And because of it, the king's heart was moved to compassion and overruled the edict of death that was on her people. Esther had a strategy. She was a true Warrior Bride, who was not moved by her emotions – nor did she react to circumstances, but was patient in battle. The first time with the king, she gained ground. The second time, she gained more ground. The third time, she had the victory, but it took her tears! The king overturned the edict, and a nation was saved, because of one person's sacrificial love, and explicit and absolute obedience to the counsel of the Lord, which enabled her to touch the heart of God, causing His plans to come forth.

Tears are not often easy. They do not come easily for most, because our hearts are too hard. But when the destruction comes, it will be easy to cry many tears, but it will be too late! We need the tears now to appease and comfort God's heart, while there is still time to do so!

## When We Fast!

It will also take our fastings, as we saw with Esther, and with Joel calling a holy solemn assembly to come with fasting, with weeping and with mourning. Every one of the Ninevites fasted after Jonah told them that if they did not repent, Nineveh would be overthrown. When we fast, whether individually or corporately, a humbling takes place to our souls. It helps us to be truly broken over our sin, our nation's sin or a situation, where our pleadings have the ability to cause the heart of God to move from judgment to mercy, bringing life and restoration, instead of the inevitable death that would have come without our prayers, tears, intercessions and fastings.

**MATTHEW 9:14-15**
*Then the disciples of John came to Him, saying, "Why do we and the Pharisees fast often, but Your disciples do not fast?" And Jesus said to them, "Can the friends of the bridegroom mourn as long as the bridegroom is with them? But the days will come when the bridegroom will be taken away from them, and then they will fast."*

Every believer is called to fast. The Lord did not say, if we fast. He said, "...then they will fast." So it must be for our good, if the Lord says that we will do it. It is a discipline to our flesh that helps us to spiritually grow and mature. If we are to touch the heart of God, we will be a people who will fast. And, while doing so, remain like putty in His hands so His wisdom, revelation, understanding and corrections can shape and form us into what He knows we need, to keep moving forward with Him. He loves it when we stay fluid in His hands and allow Him to get the maximum benefit for why we are fasting. He loves to astound us with what only He can do in our lives, when we yield wholeheartedly to Him, and this includes our times of fasting.

**MATTHEW 6:16-18**

*Moreover, when you fast, do not be like the hypocrites, with a sad countenance. For they disfigure their faces that they may appear to men to be fasting. Assuredly, I say to you, they have their reward. But you, when you fast, anoint your head and wash your face, so that you do not appear to men to be fasting, but to your Father who is in the secret place; and your Father who sees in secret will reward you openly.*

Often believers, whether they realise it or not, try to manipulate the Lord with their fasting. They want an answer or an outcome for a situation to take place in their timing. There is nothing wrong with fasting for those things. They are good and holy and necessary at times, but we must not come into our fasting thinking that the Lord is going to give us what we want or even answer. For often, He responds to our fasts not with what we thought was needed. And sometimes the answer may not come for days, weeks or even months later.

**ISAIAH 55:8-9**

*For My thoughts are not your thoughts, nor are your ways My ways, says the Lord. For as the heavens are higher than the earth, so are My ways higher than your ways, and My thoughts than your thoughts.*

I believe the Lord honours our fastings and will not let those sacrifices be in vain. At the same time, we need to check our hearts as to the motive for our fasts. Are we promoting our kingdom building, or His? If His, then are we willing to put aside any preconceived ideas of what we think He wants to do in and through us during these times? Are we willing to be putty in His hands and let Him decide what is best for us, without putting restrictions on Him? Or, are we trying to manipulate God to get what we want? Our motives should be to want to draw near, that we may understand His ways, so they can become our ways. And for the revelation we gain to transform us to become more compatible with Him in our words, thoughts and deeds.

**MARK 9:29**
*So He said to them, This kind can come out by nothing but prayer and fasting.*

Our fasting is needed to break strongholds and to set captives free. There are certain demonic oppressions in a person's life that will not be driven out, unless we pray and fast. In those situations, our fastings are specific, and will bring us the counsel and strategy that is needed in how to drive out the demonic [Mark 9:29].

### Eternal Purpose

Whether I do a one-day, three-day, ten-day, 14-day, 21-day or 40-day fast, I always ask the same thing, *"Lord, let every eternal purpose for why I am doing this fast be fulfilled."* Sometimes my fasts are voluntary; others He calls me to them. They are all by His grace alone. In either case, I often will feel the unction to set time apart for fasting, but rarely do I have a request of the Lord, other than for me to know Him and to be positioned for whatever it is He knows that I need to accomplish His plans for my life.

For example, when the Lord called me to move to Ireland, I had purposed to do a 40-day fast with the sole purpose, that every eternal purpose for why He was moving me to this nation would be fulfilled. I did not have any idea of what that might be, but knew I needed His help in every way possible. I thought I would be here a year or two, interceding for the land. But towards the end of that fast, the Lord revealed the call that I was to raise up 32 Houses of Prayer, one in every county. I can assure you that was not on my radar at all! And I will add that there is nothing in the natural that makes it possible for me to do so, but nothing is impossible with God!

There are times when I will set time apart to fast for a new assignment, or a new realm of authority that He has given to me, in order for it to be consecrated to Him, so His will can be done, and not mine. A book I highly recommend is *Rees Howells – Intercessor*.[19] I believe it should be required reading for anyone who has been called and bears His name. Reese Howells was a part of the Welsh Revival and his accountings of his surrendered life and times of fasting to the Lord are truly awe inspiring!

**Isaiah 56:7**
*Even them I will bring to My holy mountain, and make them joyful in My house of prayer. Their burnt offerings and their sacrifices will be accepted on My altar; for My house shall be called a house of prayer for all nations.*

## Eleventh Hour Laborers

In a recent message, Pastor Joe Sweet, *Shekinah Worship Center*, shared how every move of God has been birthed through humility, desperation – a hunger, and prayer. And every move has been lost due to pride and selfish ambition that caused strife and division.

Beloved, we are the best wine that has been saved for last. We are the eleventh-hour laborers. If we are to be the Bride of Messiah, who will touch the heart of God, we must intentionally make our lives a house of prayer with our prayers, tears, intercessions and fastings. We cannot afford for our homes, churches and ministries not to be a house of prayer for all nations, where everything that we do is birthed from that place of pure prayer.

We cannot afford to run the race that is set before us, leaning on our flesh, and in selfish ambition, or to compete against one another, anymore. If we do, we will disqualify ourselves and miss being a part of the greatest move of God in all of His history that is about to manifest in the nations to bring in the great harvest. Those who are making themselves ready, by keeping their loins girded with truth and their lamps burning with pure, intimate prayer with the Lover of their soul, are going to emerge, walking in unoffended love, clothed in His Light and filled with His glory.

This Bridal company is going to be the greatest testimony of His name, His love, His mercy and His miracle working powers that have not been seen before on earth. Through these exploits, ultimately, Yeshua will be crowned King over the nations. He will receive the fruit of the travail of His soul, and He will be satisfied in His Bride. Are you willing? Is your family and nation not worth fighting for? Is the Lord not worthy of all of our love, adorations, time, affections, devotions, praise, worship and thanksgivings? May the Bride of Messiah unite, arise and rebuild the broken-down walls that need rebuilding, so that our nations may be saved. For on that Day, His Bride will crown Him King over the nations, as He alone deserves! AMEN!

# CHAPTER 8

# CLEAN HANDS
# & A PURE HEART

*Who may ascend into the hill of the Lord? Or who may stand in His holy place? He who has clean hands and a pure heart, who has not lifted up his soul to an idol, nor sworn deceitfully. Blessed are the pure in heart, for they shall see God* [Psalm 24:3-4, Matthew 5:8].

When the Israelites had been freed from Egypt, God told them they were to be a kingdom of priests and a holy nation. He then told Moses to consecrate the people for three days. They were to be set apart and be holy unto the Lord. During that time, in their unclean state, they were not to touch the mountain. If they did, they were to be put to death. After three days, the mountain was covered in smoke, lightning and thunder. The Lord then gave them the ten commandments. The people, in fear, stood afar off and told Moses they did not want God to speak to them directly. Instead, they wanted him to tell them what God spoke, because of their fear. God wanted to meet with His people directly, but on His terms and they were not willing. Moses tried to alleviate their fear but they chose to stand afar off. It was not God's will for them [Exodus 19, 20].

It is the same today for many in the Body. It is the Father's will for all of us to come into that deep, pure, intimate place where we may know Him and be able to touch His heart clothed in our priestly garments. For it is only with clean hands and a pure, undivided heart that anyone is allowed to touch the heart of God. The invitation is to all, but few are willing to pay the price, as it will cost a person everything of self, if they say, "Yes" to the Bride's invite. For He is a holy God, Who will not mix His holiness with our filth.

## The Hour is Late

And at the same time, we must walk in unoffended love. When we take offense with one another – being critical, not thinking the best of each other with sin in our heart, we will not be able to discern correctly good from evil. Our flesh will lead us astray every time, we will make wrong decisions. The hour is late. We cannot afford to let the lens of our unhealed wounds or trauma cause us to view ourselves or others in a way that is not truth. When we do, we hurt ourselves and the eternal relationships that God has for us. We become blind and deaf and miss the eternal purposes for our lives.

But every unhealed wound and offense can be fully healed and cleansed, if we are willing to crucify our flesh to what we think we need. Often, though, we are just too selfish to die to self. For there can be a comfort we find in what is familiar, even if it is toxic to our relationships. If we continue to hold onto those wounds, trauma and offenses, we will eventually make them into idols within our souls. We will drive ourselves out of the presence of God.

**1 Peter 5:6**
*Therefore humble yourselves under the mighty hand of*
*God, that He may exalt you in due time,*

It will become very hard to enter into prayer and our prayer life will dry up. Why? Because we have undealt sin or wounds in our hearts, making them hard towards the Lord and others. And if not dealt with His way, we will end up walking further away from Him, when we need to be turning towards Him. Until we humble ourselves before Him and others, we will keep finding fault with those around us, not wanting to look at the log in our own eyes. But when we repent, or seek the healing and deliverance that we need, He brings restoration to our souls.

**ACTS 3:19**
*Repent therefore and be converted, that your sins may be blotted out, so that times of refreshing may come from the presence of the Lord,*

## Lover of Our Souls

Prayer is a love relationship with the Lover of our souls. If our prayer life is suffering and we find it hard to enter into prayer on a regular basis, then something is not right in our relationship with the Lord. He is not the problem, we are. We can either ignore it and keep running away from Him with all of our excuses, or let Him do what He wants in our hearts and lives – no matter how humbling or painful it may feel at the time. Our pride will usually scream the loudest!

Why am I saying this? Because prayer is the way He chose to communicate with His creation. Prayer is vital if we are to have a healthy relationship with Him and each other. Prayer is our hope for the dark days to come. Beloveds, things are going to get much harder in the days to come as we see communism, censorship, the central bank digital currency and artificial intelligence plaguing our nations, all leading to the implementation of the Mark of the Beast. If your prayer life is less than stellar, you will not be hearing correctly. You will make decisions that take you out of the Father's will for your life and could possibly end your life prematurely.

**LUKE 9:35 AMP.**
*Then there came a voice out of the cloud, saying, this is My Son, My Chosen One or My Beloved; listen to and yield to and obey Him!*

We must be a people of obedience. It bears repeating, that there is nothing more important than to hear and obey the voice of the Lord in our lives. Our Father in heaven desires that we do. He desires that we do, so we will walk worthy of His Son by doing what He asked us to do. Yeshua spent most of the night in prayer, hearing what the Father wanted Him to do for the day that was ahead of Him. We must constantly run to Him and not away from Him. For it is in that place of prayer and waiting on Him where we will hear counsel, receive instruction and accept corrections, so that we may be wise in the time to come and know how to conduct our lives on this earth, and walk as the Lord walked on this earth [Proverbs 19:20].

We must be a humble and meek people. For He leads the humble in what is right and teaches the humble His ways. True Kingdom authority is clothed in the robe of humility and meekness. Without it, pride will cause us to fall every time, causing us to fall far from the heart of God.

## He Draws Even Closer

We must be an intimate people, who draws near to the Lover of our soul. For when we do, He draws even closer to us. If we want an intimate relationship with the Lord and be able to hear and discern correctly, then we must not only obey and be humble, but make dedicated time for prayer, studying the Word and dedicated time to wait on Him. For the Bride of Messiah is a Bride of intimacy. She will learn to hear His voice when she dwells in the secret place of the Most High. And that secret place is found when we learn to abide in love. When we do, we will stay attached to the Vine, where intimacy is developed, nurtured, matured and maintained.

> **COLOSSIANS 1:9-11**
> *For this reason we also, since the day we heard it, do not cease to pray for you, and to ask that you may be filled with the knowledge of His will in all wisdom and*

*spiritual understanding; that you may walk worthy of the Lord, fully pleasing Him, being fruitful in every good work and increasing in the knowledge of God; strengthened with all might, according to His glorious power, for all patience and long suffering with joy;*

We must be a people who seek Him wholeheartedly, loving Him with all of our heart, soul, mind and strength by constantly having our mind renewed. So that we may be filled with the knowledge of His will in all wisdom and spiritual understanding, that we will know the perfect will of the Father for our lives. When we do, we will not miss the blessed opportunities to be shaped and formed into His likeness. We will not miss seeing the God of heaven take what the enemy wanted to destroy us with, and use it for our good. We will be prepared, armed and engaged in the battle that is raging all around us. And while doing so, we will not lose heart, grow weary or faint along the way.

We must become a people who walk in holiness, living a lifestyle of holiness, where our lives are 100% consecrated—set apart, for His eternal purposes. When we do, we will want the Refiner's fire to come and burn up the dross in our souls and all the wood, hay and stubble now. We will become vessels of noble use, who are prepared to do any good work the Master desires to do in and through us, and we will not lose any of our eternal rewards. We will become vessels of mercy that have been prepared beforehand that will display His glory in these last days.

We must learn to become a faithful people full of faith. For without faith and faithfulness it is not possible to be the Bride of Messiah. But when we walk in faithfulness, we will willingly come out of Babylon and put away all our other lovers that we had hidden in our hearts, that crowded Him out. We will come back to that place of undivided devotion, with dove's eyes only for the King of kings and Lord of lords. We will overcome by the blood of the Lamb, by the words of our testimonies and not love our lives, unto death.

## The Call

We must be a people of prayers, tears, intercessions and fastings. The call is to all. It is not for a few select. All are called, but few are chosen because of the choices they make. It is a choice to discipline our flesh, to come low and broken before a holy God with clean hands and a pure heart. It is a call to walk in obedience, humility and stay teachable that we can receive correction, without taking offense by the constant renewal of our minds. It is a call to spend time in the weeping room where we will decrease, that we may fit through the holy door that leads to the strategy room.

When we do, we will come before Him with clean hands and a pure heart and be able to touch His high and lofty noble heart, because it is no longer us who live but Messiah living in and through us. And not for our sakes and selfish gains, but all for the Lamb's sake. For the Lamb to receive the reward of His suffering as He deserves in a Bridal company, who considers Him worth knowing, by willing to pay any price to be made ready for the Wedding Supper of the Lamb. AMEN!

# ENDNOTES


1   https://www.dictionary.com/browse/purity.

2   Tracy Hogan, *The Days of Noah*, https://thevoiceofmybeloved.com/
    teachings-intercessors-for-ireland/, https://www.youtube.com/
    watch?v=FQkIqMoKp-E, (The Voice of My Beloved, April 2018).

3   Dr. Michael L. Brown, Craig S. Keener, *Not Afraid of the Antichrist:
    Why We Don't Believe in a Pre-Tribulation Rapture*, (Chosen Books,
    March 19, 20219).

4   *Strong's Concordance*, 3618.

5   *Strong's Concordance*, 3634.

6   *National Geographic Article: Kingdom*, https://education.
    nationalgeographic.org/resource/kingdom/
    (accessed April 13, 2023).

7   Tracy Hogan, *Bewitched & Beguiled: Wolves in Sheep's Clothing*,
    (The Voice of My Beloved, 2021).

8   *Blue Letter Bible Lexicon*, Strong's G3754.

9   Nita Johnson, *World for Jesus Ministries*, author's notes from
    one of the Gathering of the Eagles teaching sessions.

10  *Collins Dictionary*, https://www.collinsdictionary.com/
    dictionary/english/embrace (accessed May 7,2023).

11  Kenneth E. Hagin, *I Believe in Visions*, (Tulsa, OK: Rhema
    Bible Church, fifth edition) 75-82.

12  https://www.vocabulary.com/dictionary/faithful, https://www.collinsdictionary.com/dictionary/english/faithful, https://www.collinsdictionary.com/dictionary/english/faithful (accessed April 25, 2023).

13  https://en.wikipedia.org/wiki/Betrayal, https://www.dictionary.com/browse/betrayal (accessed April 25, 2023).

14  https://www.christianity.com/wiki/prayer/prayer-of-petition-when-seeking-gods-help.html (accessed April 30, 2023).

15  https://www.blueletterbible.org/faq/don_stewart/don_stewart_543.cfm (accessed April 30, 2023).

16  Mike Bickle, *International House of Prayer University*, Free Teaching Library: www.mikebickle.org

17  Tracy Hogan, *Bewitched & Beguiled: Wolves in Sheep's Clothing*, (The Voice of My Beloved, 2021) 136-137.

18  Jennifer Miller Toledo, *The Weeping Room – Pathway to Strategy* vision, 2004.

19  Norman P. Grubb, *Rees Howells – Intercessor*, (Lutterworth Press, Guildford and London, 1973).

# ABOUT THE AUTHOR

Ever since the return to the love of her life, the Lord Yeshua, in 1999, Tracy Hogan has walked closely and intimately with the One whom her soul loveth and adores. In 2007 she had a life-changing experience where the Lord allowed her to witness some end-times events. In 2009 the Lord came and awakened her in a different way, by revealing His high and holy standards of what it means to be pure in His eyes and just how pure one's heart has to be if they are to see His Face. It jolted her to the core. It was the beginning of her journey to become His Bride.

Tracy's call is to the nations. She prophetically teaches the Word of God to help prepare the Bride of Messiah for the Lord Yeshua's soon coming return. For her to know how to dress herself in her wedding garments – to be a Bride who has made herself ready – one who will be without spot or wrinkle, and one who will be ready for her wedding day. This bridal preparation comes by teaching her truth, purity, holiness, and in helping nurture in her an intimate love relationship with our Bridegroom King through worship, intercession and warfare.

Tracy resides in Ireland, where she founded The Voice of My Beloved – A Call to the Nations Ministry.

*The Voice of My Beloved*

A Call to the Nations Ministry

www.thevoiceofmybeloved.com

www.ingramcontent.com/pod-product-compliance
Lightning Source LLC
Chambersburg PA
CBHW050941050726
47592CB00007B/2386